Stop Spinning Plates

**How to Lose
Your Balance and
Become a Thriving
Mother**

Susan Guiher and Mary McHenry

Denver, Colorado
FIRST EDITION
© 2007

Success Circle Coaching
PO Box 813
Nederland, CO 80466

Printed in the United States of America. 10 9 8 7 6 5 4 3 2 1

Library of Congress Catalog Card Number: 2007908801

Guiher, Susan
McHenry, Mary
        Stop Spinning Plates

        Includes bibliography and appendix.

The content and opinions expressed in this book are the sole work of the authors, editors and publishers who have warranted due diligence in the creation and issuance of their work. The publisher, editors, and authors are not responsible for errors or omissions or for any consequences arising from the information or opinions presented in this book and make no warranty, expressed or implied, with respect to its contents.

Cover Design and Layout: Sylvie Abecassis

ISBN 0-9786058-2-9

Dedication

To the strong, vulnerable, resilient spirit of the mother who thrives in all of us.
To my mother, Frances Boatner McHenry for being my lifelong teacher.
And to Jeffrey and Luke, who bring out the best in me.
With much love and gratitude,
MMcH

To my mother, Nancy Armitage Conrad, who has supported me to
become the best Mom I can be. To Mike who encourages and
inspires me on a daily basis and to Matthew, Christopher and
Meghan for the honor of letting me be their mother.
With much love and appreciation,
SCG

In Memory:
To our fathers, Frederick Charles Conrad, Jr. and
Robert William McHenry, Sr.,
who instilled integrity, strength and an
entrepreneurial spirit in both of us. We miss you!

Acknowledgements

Now we know how very true the rumor is – it DOES take a village to write a book!

We want to express our immense gratitude to everyone who helped us birth this baby. We'll try to touch on you all here:

This book started a few years ago as interviews with women who were mothers and were having great success in network marketing, and the difference it was making for them and for their family's financial health. The next version was interviews again, this time with mothers with varied home businesses. We have evolved away from the stories to this hands-on workbook on Thriving, but none of this would have been possible without the amazing lives, experience and willingness to share that these women gave:

Valerie White (partner along part of the journey), Kathy Duvall, Yvonne Senay, Julie Abarzua, Aoife Gaffney, Bridget Fearing, Heather Novak, Michelle Brookhaus, Sheryl Pause, Mary Button, Gea Franklin, Catherine Camp, Jennifer Turco, Kathy Monet-Smith, Beth Landry-Murphy, Milana Leshinsky, Laurie Rasch, Sue Talbert, and Jeanne McCauley.

Please find excerpts of many of these women's stories in the Appendix B and on our website at www.successcirclecoaching.com/interviews. More tales to come!

Thank you to Tara Gray Wolfstar (aka Spider) for juicy artwork assistance, and to Sylvie Abecassis for the gorgeous book you hold in your hands right now.

To Sarah Lateer for her fast fingered transcriptions and Lisa Miles Brady for her faith in us and for asking great questions.

A huge heartfelt thank you to James Purcaro for his generosity and patience in the printing of this book, and for being the catalyst for dream manifestation that he is in the world. YOU ROCK!!

Tremendous gratitude to the original members of the *Thriving Mothers' Community*: Bridget Fearing, Heather Novak, Christy Venters, Donna Coulter, Jeannie Zandi and all the other women who stopped in when they could! Your participation in the calls, enthusiasm for the connection of the group and your "testing" of the tools has been invaluable to the creation of this book. You are truly the inspiration for how this whole thing has evolved.

Mary

I turn my heart and soul to thank Jeffrey for knowing and believing in me, completely; and Luke for asking "Mom, did you finish chapter 13 yet?", and other encouraging questions. I want to thank my big brother Bob who handed me his first published book, when I was only 10, and sparked the dream and desire in me to be a published author someday. And Keith and Lorraine Fairmont, who welcomed sleepovers, watched all the kids and made blueberry pancakes while I did edits in the basement!

My heart goes out to my amazing women friends, especially Lori and Leda for backing me up on anything and everything. Huge appreciation to the women's communities in my life, including the Mountain Divas hockey group for full out physical play (great for writer's block!); and to the Mountain Goddesses Book Club for their intellect, good food, encouragement and willingness to read manuscripts! To Annie, Michael and Christa for seeing who I am and cheering me on. And to the women of my mastermind teams: Lyn, Sherry, Heather, Michelle, Amanda and Rita – together we are modeling the kind of support that is at the very foundation of this book.

Sue

I would like to thank Mike for his commitment to this project and to me and also for his encouragement of my mini writing retreats. Also to Matt, Chris and Meghan who remind me that thriving looks and feels different every single day and who make my heart sing on a daily basis.

I wish to thank Bev for her lifelong friendship, Rachna for her steadfast friendship, Irene for being an original thriving mother and showing me the way and to Beth for watching the kids to give me some errand time and listening to me talk about "the book" all summer. You are all amazing blessings in my life.

A very personal thank you goes to Lynne Klippel for your friendship, encouragement and mentorship in the book writing and marketing process. A big thanks also to Michael Port and Terri Levine for your encouragement, wisdom and mentorship.

Thank you also to Kim Burrows for opening the Justa Farm Dream Dinners (and saving many family nights) and to Karyn, Lisa, Sue and Sarah who were always there to help get me more of something to make my meals. Thanks to Trish for joining me every month to make our meals together and share our lives. Our friendship continues to evolve and I am grateful for that.

To Jodi Golub and Carol Mc Kay for your proofreading eyes and inspiring comments along the journey.

I would also like to thank the New Hope Chapter members of BNI and the ladies of the Eve Circle who encouraged me on a regular basis and asked "how's the book coming". And tremendous appreciation also to the members of my coaching circles and my clients who remind me why I am so passionate about coaching, writing and creating a thriving life.

There are many more of you. Your names are in our hearts,

Mary and Sue

Eldora, Colorado and Ivyland, Pennsylvania

October, 2007

Contents

Introduction

Stand by your convictions!
Remember the mighty Oak is just a nut
who stood her ground.
— Folk Wisdom

The Birth of the Book

This book began as a great conversation and a desire to collaborate. We were discussing a book project Mary was working on featuring interviews with successful work at home mothers. The inspiration for the book was that these stories would inspire other women and support them in their choice to work from home. Mary expressed her longing for a partner in this project. As she described this book, it sounded very much like a project Sue had been working on two years prior and had stopped because she had wanted a partner and had not found the perfect one at the time.

So, our partnership was forged. What is really amazing and cool is that our collaboration thrives even though we live on opposite sides of the United States, experience different lifestyles and have different backgrounds. Our conversations, with each other and with other women, continue to flow – deepening and expanding as we tap into the roots of our shared values and visions.

What started as a dialogue about Mompreneurship has gone way beyond that. We started saying — the heck with surviving, the heck with balancing – what would the world be like if we thrived! What if it began with us — women and mothers, such a powerful force on the planet?   What if how we treat ourselves and each other ripples out to change the lives of our children and grandchildren for the better?

True, sustainable thriving is not just about feeling good — it's about living into our potential and calling out the very best in us. With this book, we invite you to walk along with us in this journey of possibility, for you, for all of us.

The Tales of Two Thriving Mothers

Mary

The more I look into it, the more I recognize how profoundly mothers have shaped my life. Not only my own mother, but her relationship with her mother, the stories about grandmothers and aunts on both sides of my family, and the messages I've picked up about motherhood since I was a very small girl. Way before I was a mother myself. Even when I thought I'd never be a mom.

I was the last of five children in my family. My mother was almost 40 in 1960 when she finally had me — her only girl. My brothers were 16, 12, 10 and 8 when I was born, so I grew up in a tribe of baby boomer boys. All the 1950's modes of motherhood were in full swing. My mother never worked, and her art was always "just a hobby". My father was the breadwinner and as a young child, I never gave this arrangement a second thought.

As I came of age in the 1970's, though, I rejected this scenario full out. The cultural messages to a budding young woman shifted drastically from my experience growing up. The swell of women's rights, feminism and radical change were protesting in one ear. (One of my friend's mothers even held Girl's Consciousness Raising meetings for us.) My housewife mother grabbed desperately for her girl child's attention in the other ear.

I chose freedom, baby. At least what I thought freedom was.

This journey to "freedom" is material for another book. To make a long story short, my rebellion of motherhood and convention was so ingrained that I was 39 before I had my one and only son. Many women of my generation waited until just under the wire to start a family. I remember having a great laugh at a greeting card I saw in that 50's cartoon style of a woman grimacing with her hand on her forehead that read "Oh my gosh, I forgot to have children!"

Of course, when Luke was born, my heart burst open with love and I couldn't believe I had waited one single day for a miracle like him. And after a bumpy transition of a couple of years, I have fallen deeply in love with motherhood, too.

As I traveled this path I began to see how my rebellion no longer served. The world is a different place than it was in the 70's. I'm a little older and wiser, too. Yet something remains from that revolutionary time, and part of what's hanging out there is the question of what to **do** with our freedom as women.

There is an undercurrent of anxiety and angst these days. It feels like it's not okay for us to love staying home with our kids if we have talent to share with the world. And then when we're out in the world doing it, it's sort of not okay to be away from our kids. In subtle and sometimes not so subtle ways we are often apologizing for ourselves.

So maybe it's not rebellion that's needed, but a revolution. Not a battle, but a coming- back-around kind of revolution, like the earth revolves. Maybe in this way we'll remember how to thrive. How to be free.

I've treasured my journey of becoming an entrepreneur, because it has allowed me to grow into my work in the world in a very personal way. From this springs my passion for working with other women entrepreneurs on their journeys. I deeply believe that together, we can mother the world, the marketplace, our kids and each other in the highest possible way — nurturing, encouraging and stewarding us all toward thriving.

Sue

I grew up in a "traditional family" in a middle class suburb of Philadelphia. I was born in the mid 60's and have an older and younger brother. My father went off to work every day and I remember as a young girl waiting for him to return from work. My mother's work life was varied and different. I found out as an adult that she worked for many years in a large company prior to marrying my father and up until she was 6 months pregnant with my older brother.

My mom stayed home with the kids until I was in 6th grade and my older brother was going off to college. She re-entered the work force to help supplement the family income so my brother could attend the college of his choice. At the time, I think I saw her work as not as "important" as my father's because it was part-time and not a "career". My younger brother and I even resented a little bit that she was not home with us as much as she had been.

Though truth be told, neither my brothers nor myself would have been able to pursue our careers had it not been for my Mom re-entering the work force. As I went off to college, she then did have a career that lasted many years. I saw how much she grew in that job and how she managed to combine working with having a family.

"My life changed having seen the moon on the other side of the world".

The 70's also influenced my choices as I entered adulthood. I saw the commercials for the Super Moms who could work and then come home to their families and DO IT ALL. That was the message I received and believed. I fully intended to continue working and, as I kept climbing the corporate ladder, this message was playing full-blast in my ear. I saw other women in management working and raising a family and trying to **BALANCE** it all. I also kept noticing how tired they seemed to be.

I married, continued to work and had a very successful career. When I became pregnant with my first child, Matthew, the message was getting a little louder. "You can do it all, you can work and be a successful mother and wife. You have all these college degrees; you can't "waste them".

Then an amazing thing happened. I fell in love with my son and thought — "How can I leave him all day?" — How can I work 60 hour work weeks and then come home and give him what he needs?" During my maternity leave, I had an amazing experience that truly changed me. My husband, Mike, had to work in Switzerland for a month during my leave, so Matthew (who was 2 months at the time) and I went with him.

I often say, "My life changed having seen the moon on the other side of the world". I spent that month bonding with Matt and taking him everywhere I went. We visited museums and cathedrals and attended events and dinners.
It was fabulous, and really made me realize that I wanted more than just work and a career. I wanted to learn more about other cultures and wanted to share this with my children. At the same time I still wanted to help support my family and still use my skills. Working from home became the right choice for all of us and eight years (and now three children) later, I am still convinced that this was the right choice.

The road has not always been an easy or smooth one.
I seemed to be in good company because at the same time I choose to stay at home, so did many of my friends who also

had very successful careers. For some reason, we all felt like we were letting "someone" down by staying home. We felt like we were wasting our talents and needed to apologize for our decision to raise our children.

The messages of our childhood were coming back at us loud and clear. The more I coach women to make the choices that are right for them, the more passionate I become about women not apologizing for their decisions. I also realize the only way to do this is to create a place of understanding; a place where all women can stand together and thrive. If every woman would take a moment from her busy life, stop and breathe and then turn to another woman and support her unconditionally in her desire to thrive, we would change the world. Plain and simple. I invite you to take this journey with us to find your place to thrive.

This is an invitation to interact and converse, rather than debate and be right.

Stepping Up On Our Soapbox

We both grew up with the model of the Super Mom. Remember the commercial jingle "I can bring home the bacon, fry it up in the pan and never never never let you forget you're a man, 'cause I'm a woman…." We can feel that message shifting, but to what?

Now, that is what we want explore with you in this book. Let's stop spinning plates and take a look at moving to a more sustainable way of being. We are inspired to open these avenues of dialogue and conversation because we feel that there has been too much debate and conflict between Moms who make the choice to stay home with their children and Moms who choose to work outside the home.*

We've been stunned recently by the so called Mommy Wars – a name-calling spat cheered on by the media that pits working mothers against stay at home mothers. Why are we stunned? First: there is no mention of work at home mothers in this battle – even when current statistics reveal that greater than 11 million women own and run a business from home (according to the Direct Sellers Association). It really isn't just an either/or thing anymore — it's a both/and thing!

And second: Why are we calling this choice (or necessity) a war? What good can possibly come from that? What good has ever come from that? This book, and the Thriving Mothers' Community we are creating, offer the opportunity for support and collaboration. This is an invitation to interact and converse, rather than debate and be right.

We will highlight women who have made the choice to work from home and what insights they have had along

···

You may see these groups referred to as:
SAHMs — Stay At Home Moms
WOHMs — Work Outside the Home Moms
WAHMs — Work At Home Moms

the way. (See Appendix B) So, allow us to step on our soapbox for a moment: Working from home and having your own business is a huge consideration in our Thriving Motherhood model.

It is not for everyone, we know. We've coached a lot of folks between the two of us, and a handful find out they are just not cut out to be business owners. We respect that there is a very diverse array of circumstances out there among women. We still have to sing entrepreneurship's praises right here. It's worth your consideration. For those who have the desire and the opportunity to work from home, the list of amazing advantages to Mompreneurship is huge.

Here are just a few:

⊙ Flexibility to set your own hours, tasks, pace, client load and way of doing business;
⊙ Setting a very real example for your children that making a living has many possibilities and can be enjoyable;
⊙ Offering an experiential learning environment in which children can explore their own entrepreneurial instincts;
⊙ Creating work that values your skills, talents, visions, dreams and capabilities. – making a life, not just a living.

When we become parents, we are powerful examples to our kids. We have the opportunity (over and over again) to practice, be aware of, and choose how we do what we do. This includes how we relate to our work and make a living. We get the chance to live into it. Our work can be juicy, rich, and fulfilling. We can show our kids that our work is only a part of who we are and how we spend our time.

Working at home can create a place to blend all parts of our lives – family, home, work, self, community and spiritual life. May this book serve as a guide to support you to create that place for you and your family, whether you work from home or not.

Please accept our thank you gift at
www.stopspinningplates.com/thankyougifts

CHAPTER 1

Stop Spinning Plates!

Get the kids to sport's practice – SPIN
Figure out what's for dinner – SPIN
Write and send out newsletter – SPIN

Spend some time with husband – SPIN
Remember to send brother's birthday card – SPIN
Figure out how to bring in two more clients – SPIN

OOPS Take the dog to the vet – SPIN SPIN
DARN! The post office just closed – SPIN SPIN SPIN
Find time for me – S P I . . . .

Sound Familiar?

If this sounds like your life, congratulations and welcome!
You are not alone in this crazy, stressful dance of trying to
keep all those plates in the air.

You are hereby invited to stop striving to balance all the
areas of your life. Yup. Stop balancing! We will stand by
you as you begin to create a life for you and your family
that thrives.

Not even sure what that could look like?   That's okay. This is
a journey. The tools and resources in this book, along with

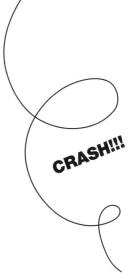

CRASH!!!

the Thriving Mothers' Community, are here to support and guide you. If you are ready to stop spinning the plates of your life, we invite you to settle in and use this book as a resource and a guide to creating something different.

Who is this for?

Our inspiration for this project began with Mompreneurs — Moms who own their own business or who are thinking about starting their own business. However, as we talked and shared the information with other Moms — Stay At Home Moms (SAHMs), Work Outside the Home Moms (WOHMs) as well as Work At Home Moms (WAHMs), we found that we all had things in common. All the women we spoke with felt they were spinning plates, juggling too much or stressed out to some degree. We even heard from women who were not Moms who wanted in on this community. So, while much of the voice of this book will be speaking to WAHMs, our intention is to help all women go from a place of striving to a place of thriving.

It's choice
– not chance –
that determines
your destiny.
— Jean Nidetch

Why Not Balance?

We are not saying that balance is a bad thing. In fact, if we think of it as finding harmony or experiencing equilibrium, it's a wonderful thing. Dr Wayne Dyer, in his book, *Being in Balance: 9 Principles for Creating Habits to Match Your Desires,* says that all other creatures in the universe except humans are inherently in balance. He goes on to say, "one of the huge imbalances in life is the disparity between your daily existence and the dream you have deep within yourself of some extraordinarily satisfying way of living."

Here's the rub — trying to achieve balance feels so stressful! For women these days, it often means juggling all areas of your life at all times and looking good while you're doing it. Balance has become that elusive place we are supposed to attain (and hold) and are never quite able to. We are bombarded with messages that doing it all is the key to our family's happiness. We seem to be using this definition of "balance" against ourselves as a weapon.

Today it seems like every woman's magazine wants to show us how to get it right. There is every expert wanting to tell us exactly how we, too, can master "the work/life balance". You have seen the articles — The 7 Secrets to Having Balance or How to Balance your Business and Your Marriage or BLAH BLAH BLAH. **ENOUGH!!!** This message needs to change. It DOESN'T work!! The plates just end up crashing down and we feel tired, alone, guilty and not good enough.

There are a lot of women out there feeling this way- we know, *we* felt this way and we have heard from you that you often feel this way too. We've been sitting on a seesaw trying to get both sides completely balanced. Finally it gets there. Then what happens? Something in your life changes, *boom*, the seesaw tips. You have to stay still in order to stay balanced. Good luck!

The New Message

The new message is this: Become the center of your life. Take back control and create a life based on your values and your vision. Blend all the areas of your life in a way that allows you and your family to grow, develop, change, and make mistakes so you can all THRIVE.

You can become a Thriving Mother. Thriving as a mom is a process and a journey, not really an event or a completed project. It's something you practice being, not something you check off your to-do list. We like to say we are thriving mothers in creation. We are on the Thriving Mother's Path.

The definition of thriving as given by the Merriam-Webster On-line Dictionary is to *"grow vigorously"* and also to *"progress toward or realize a goal despite of or because of circumstances."* We like this definition of thriving because it allows us to continue to develop, learn, make mistakes and have "do-overs", while keeping in sight the goal of having a happy and successful life for our families and ourselves. There's no struggle to thrive the "right way".

Tools and Community

We have used the tools in this book to create very successful businesses and home lives. We have used these tools with members of our Thriving Mothers' Community on our weekly calls and they have made huge changes in their lives and the lives of their families. We want you to be successful – by finding your own definition of success.

This book will provide you with resources, both here between these covers and through your free membership in the *Thriving Mothers Community* that you will learn more about in this book. *Stop Spinning Plates* is meant to be a workbook, a journal and a means of support. There are examples throughout to guide and inspire you.

The Thriving Mother's Community Call has been a bright spot in my week. The simple act of committing just one hour a week to focus on me was a huge first step. This step led to other steps: creatively finding time to focus on my health, making time to work on my business, and finding the courage to say no to some of my biggest time drainers. In the end, I found that I got more enjoyment out of my time with my husband and son because in the back of my mind I wasn't thinking, "When do I get a break."

Christy Venters, Silpada Representative

You've Got a Friend

You will be on this journey with a virtual friend- her name is "Beth Ann" and she is a composite of Mary and Susan's stories and lives. She is truly a Thriving Mother in creation and hopefully her examples will help you in your journey.

This book is about creating a way of harmony and thriving so you can have peace and happiness as a foundation in your life — something you can always return to. We invite you to leave behind the spinning plates and the seesaw and create your own space to flourish.

Key Ideas for Thriving

- You are now part of a community of woman who are here to support and inspire you.
- Thriving is a process and a journey, not an event.
- You can create a life of harmony and more peace.
- Stop trying to balance it all by trying to keep all the plates of your life spinning in the air and look forward to something new.

Next Steps

Grab a pen or pencil because you are about to create your own *Personal Thriving Sphere*^{SM}

CHAPTER 2

Your Personal Thriving Sphere

> I was always looking outside myself for strength and confidence, but it comes from within. It is there all the time.
> — Anna Freud

Creating a Life that Thrives

There have been experiments done in which one group of plants have been given all the water and sunlight they need, but no attention at all. The second group of plants were given all the water and sunlight they need, plus lots of attention. This second group of plants thrived. What made the difference was focus and attention. This is an invitation to turn your attention to the center of who you are, and give yourself the gift of witnessing, acknowledgement and focus.

What does a thriving life look like and how do you create one? Well, it will look different for each woman. What will be common will be the experience that **you** are at the center of your life -- you are in control of how you spend your time and energy. Okay, please stop shaking your head in disbelief or laughing hysterically. Perhaps it has been a long time since you felt you are directing your life. Remember, this is a process. Don't expect instant transformation to happen overnight.

Let's just take the first step to look at where all your time is going now. There are 24 hours each day and 7 days in a week. To thrive, you start by valuing and being clear about how you are investing your time. Time is a most precious commodity. All we can do is practice spending it well.

Your Personal Thriving Sphere

Here is your first tool to creating a thriving life — your *Personal Thriving Sphere* SM *(PTS)*. This exercise is vital because it requires you to take an honest look at each area of your life, and how much of your time and energy is spent in each area. We developed this model to explore what supported us to become the hub of our own lives. By using the PTS we have a better grasp on what we want to be doing and how much time we want to be doing it.

The Personal Thriving Sphere SM is a map (your PTS rather than your GPS) you will use and it will evolve over the course of the book. It will help guide you to shift from scarcity thinking (otherwise known as poverty mentality) — There's not enough time/energy/money! — to a place of thriving thinking, which is has it's roots in abundance.

"I was feeling completely overwhelmed when I started working with Mary & Sue. Tools like the Personal Thriving Sphere, the personal coaching model and questioning my assumptions have helped move me out of overwhelm into truly thriving. As a mother and entrepreneur, I'm now more happy and effective than ever before."

— Bridget Fearing – Thriving Mothers Community Member

Getting Started

Let's begin — you will need at least 15 minutes of time alone. You may find it valuable to use the audio we've created to take you through this exercise. Go to www.successcirclecoaching.com/ptsaudio to listen and/or download.

We have included a sample Personal Thriving Sphere *SM* for Beth Ann at the end of this chapter. It is to serve only as an example of what a thriving mother's life may look like and not as a standard to follow. Since Beth Ann is a representation of both Sue and Mary, her sphere reflects their lives at a moment in time.

The Top 8

Step 1: List the 6-8 main areas of your life- these are the areas where you spend your time and energy. Examples may include: children, community, work, health, marriage, kids' activities, fitness, parents etc.

1. _____

2. _____

3. _____

4. _____

5. _____

6. _____

7. _____

8. _____

Step 2: Now identify how much time you are spending in each of these areas. Put a number to the closest 5%. When you total the areas you will come up with 100% of your time.

Step 3: Transfer the information from this page to your sphere. First write the date at the top. Since this is a snapshot of your life at any one moment in time, the date is very important.

Now put your name in the center circle and then place each of the areas from above in the outer circle on the blank PTS on the next page. If you have 6 or 7, that is okay- just fill in what you have. Each of the outside marks represents 10% so this will easily correspond to what you identified in step 2.

My Personal Thriving Sphere

Today is_____

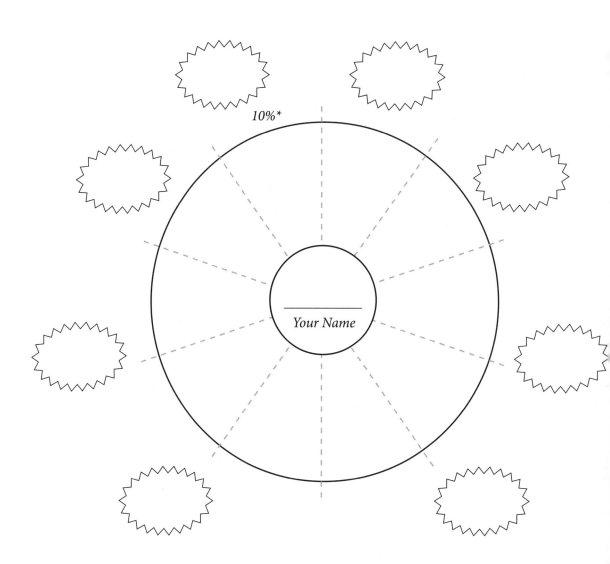

10%*

Your Name

Each section represents 10%.

What did you notice? There is no RIGHT way for your sphere to look. This is a snapshot for you to see. It will change all the time. If you feel you are spending too much time in an area and you don't feel in control of that time, that's great information. It is good to find out now where you are spending your time and how you feel about where your time is spent. Again, be very honest with yourself while doing this exercise. You will use this tool often. Spend the time to get comfortable with it.

We'll be focusing on building on your strengths in this next part of the exercise, so you'll have a solid foundation for using the PTS throughout the book and throughout your days. Shifting to this way of thinking fosters a thriving environment for you and your family. You are honoring that your life is a dynamic sphere that evolves and changes, not just a static moment.

There may be areas of your sphere you are not comfortable with and you might want to change. You may know right away how to change some areas and you might feel stuck and frustrated in others. We know. We honor that. We will be offering you tools and support to make those changes in later chapters.

Right now we'll be focusing on discovering what is working well in each area of your life, even in seemingly small ways. Begin to look for where there is harmony, ease, satisfaction or even a working system in each of your areas. The following questions will help you do that. Again you will need about 15 minutes of quiet time to go through this next exercise.

My Sphere

You are going to take each of the areas you identified in step 1 and write them below: (if you need more space, grab some paper and go for it!)

Area #1 _____

What is going well in this part of my life?

Why does this work so well for my family and me?

How does this area feel to me?

Area #2 _____

What is going well in this part of my life?

Why does this work so well for my family and me?

How does this area feel to me?

My Sphere

Area #3 _____

What is going well in this part of my life?

Why does this work so well for my family and me?

How does this area feel to me?

Area #4 _____

What is going well in this part of my life?

Why does this work so well for my family and me?

How does this area feel to me?

My Sphere

Area #5 _____

What is going well in this part of my life?

Why does this work so well for my family and me?

How does this area feel to me?

Area #6 _____

What is going well in this part of my life?

Why does this work so well for my family and me?

How does this area feel to me?

My Sphere

Area #7 _____

What is going well in this part of my life?

Why does this work so well for my family and me?

How does this area feel to me?

Area #8 _____

What is going well in this part of my life?

Why does this work so well for my family and me?

How does this area feel to me?

My Sphere

Now, look back at what you wrote in each area and select one or two key words from each area of your "What makes that work" responses. You may have the same word in more than one area. You will end up with 8-16 words.

Area 1 _____ _____

Area 2 _____ _____

Area 3 _____ _____

Area 4 _____ _____

Area 5 _____ _____

Area 6 _____ _____

Area 7 _____ _____

Area 8 _____ _____

That is what learning is.
You suddenly understand
something you've understood
all your life, but in a new way.
— Doris Lessing

Yahoo! Look what you've found! These are the clues to
your core values. These are the keys to your thriving.

We are not going to tell you what your top 10 values
should be. This is not about conforming to some ideal. In
the next chapter you will look even deeper at your values
and sort out what is really important to you and what
makes you unique. For the moment, we are sending out
an invitation for you to look at what you wrote and really
relish what is working in your life currently, to honor why
that works for you and your family and to step into the
space where you are truly being great. By taking a look at
what you are currently doing, you can identify those areas
that are working and you can enhance them even further.

Example

Beth Ann's Personal Thriving Sphere

Today is July14th, 2007

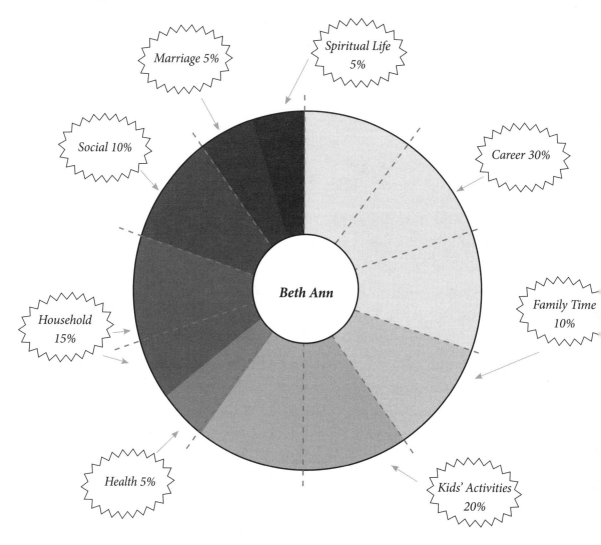

Example

Beth Ann

Area #1 Career (30%)

What is going well in this part of my life? Love writing this book, have lots of ideal clients, supporting other people to create successful lives, have a great boss (me), have flexibility to be at my kids' activities. Learning lots of new things.

Why does this work so well for my family and me? Husband is traveling a great deal this summer and away for a week+ at time so the flexibility is essential to work and take care of the kids. The opportunity to collaborate with each other and other women while writing this book is so fulfilling.

How does this area feel to me? Busy and FUN!! Creative, energizing and inspiring. Love working with people that I really enjoy and respect and have fun with.

Area #2 Family Time (10%)

What is going well in this part of my life? Having time to spend with kids this summer has been great. Because husband is away we have been creating special times when we are all together and that have been fun. We also have some "down time" together, just hanging out, which I love.

Why does this work so well for my family and me? We like to spend time together and see our children have fun with us, whether it is biking, going to a ball game, going to an amusement park or going away somewhere. Our time together is very important.

Beth Ann

How does this area feel to me? I feel calm and happy knowing that quality time is more important than the quantity of time. We have made the time really special. I'm looking forward to increasing the time on the sphere by spending a whole week together when we go away on vacation.

Area #3 Kids' Activities (20%)

What is going well in this part of my life? The kids have structured activities that they really like. They are learning new skills this summer from mountain biking to karate. They really enjoy what they have been doing and there has been some variety in their days so that they have not been bored.

Why does this work so well for my family and me. They are engaged with other kids their ages and learning new things. I love seeing them stretch themselves and grow.

How does this area feel to me? I am excited that they are learning new things and are experiencing different activities. I sometimes feel frustrated that my schedule revolves around the kids' activities. My time is limited because I have to take them to all of their activities and then wait for the activity to be complete or pick them up. It takes up a large part of my time.

Example

Beth Ann

Area #4 Health (5%)

What is going well in this part of my life? I feel pretty good. I take supplements to support my health. I feel best when I'm involved in outdoor activities. I spend time in yoga or meditation most mornings.

Why does this work so well for my family and me? The healthier and more physically active I am, the better role model I am for my family. Also I can be more involved in my kids' activities and games.

How does this area feel to me? It feels good that I can spend some time taking care of myself. I would like more time to be actively participating in a team sport or doing something else more physically challenging.

Area #5 Social (10%)

What is going well in this part of my life? I'm spending time with friends this summer; making an effort to see them. Also have friends now at kids' activities so I can socialize while they are playing their game or taking a lesson.

Why does this work so well for my family and me? I don't feel so isolated when I can get out with friends or talk to other Moms about life in general. It is also fun to be out without the kids on a "girls' night out" once a month or so.

Beth Ann

How does this area feel to me? Feels like a really vital area that supports me. I'm enjoying my friends and the people in my community.

Area #6 Household (15%)

What is going well in this part of my life? I have a house I love. I have space for an office in my home environment.

Why does this work so well for my family and me? My family loves our neighborhood and community. They can ride bikes or play. We have an incredible view of the mountains and live close to nature.

How does this area feel to me? Chores feel like they take up too much of my time -- like it's never done. I feel like I am often doing household tasks from cleaning to laundry to shopping. I want to find ways to have support and methods to make this easier.

Area #7 Spiritual (5%)

What is going well in this part of my life? Belong to a great community. Have spirituality daily in my life.

Why does this work so well for my family and me? It brings us together. Gives us a place to experience something bigger than ourselves. Also provides for traditions and rituals that are very grounding.

Example

Beth Ann

How does this area feel to me? Though given a smaller time percentage, it really feels good and even. Actually spirituality is present in almost all areas of my life so I could really blend it into them.

Area #8 Marriage (5%)

What is going well in this part of my life? Great conversations, enjoy being together.

Why does this work so well for my family and me? Creates a stronger family, support me, gives me more energy. We share a deep commitment to our family.

How does this area feel to me? Less time is being focused here because husband is away so much right now. Also have other priorities such as the writing of this book. Feels good that the time we do spend together has been spent in deep connecting. This has really helped our marriage. We've been remembering to actually **do** the things we really love to do together. Would love more "date time" with just the two of us.

Beth Ann

Beth Ann's Key Words

Area 1:   Flexibility   Creativity

Area 2:   Fun   Family

Area 3:   Learning   Active

Area 4:   Grounded   Active

Area 5:   Fun   Connected

Area 6:   Secure   Supportive environment

Area 7:   Community   Present

Area 8:   Family   Partnership

Key Ideas for Thriving

The most important concepts regarding the PTS are:

You are the center of your experience and thus in control (might not feel like it right now but that is the goal).

Your Personal Thriving Sphere is a snapshot in this moment of time of how you spend your time and this is always changing.

This is a starting point not an ending point. You will be doing more of these. We recommend that you create a fresh PTS at least on a monthly, if not weekly, basis.

You are able to make conscious changes based on what you learn from creating your PTS.

By identifying what works for you and your family and why it works, you can create more of these opportunities and spend more of your time and energy engaged in these activities.

Next Steps

We invite you to join your Thriving Mothers' Community if you have not done so already. You will be notified of our community calls and can sign up for our newsletter.

All the information is located at: www.successcirclecoaching.com

Share with us what your key words were and what was important for you. You can interact with us and other readers at our blog at www.thrivingmothers.wordpress.com. We welcome and encourage you to participate. It will add to your learning from this book

Notes

CHAPTER 3

Values

> I don't know what your destiny will be,
> but one thing I do know; the only ones among you
> who will be really happy are those who have
> sought and found how to serve.
>
> – Albert Schweitzer

Getting to the Core

Now that you've created your Personal Thriving Sphere
and examined what is working in each area of your life,
you are ready to create another map – a foundation for
what's underneath all your choices. In this chapter, you will
identify your core values and create a Thriving Values Profile.
Knowing and claiming your core values is vital for a thriving
life, largely because they support you in making decisions
that are right and true for you. We will talk more about this
once you complete the exercise.

The Values Exercise

This exercise can be done either by listening to the audio
we've provided, or by reading the list of values. We
recommend using the audio, as we have found this to be the
more effective method. If you are unable to access the audio,

you may ask someone to read the words to you, so that the exercise moves along at a good pace and you don't get stuck in thinking too long about each step.

The Values exercise is available in audio at www.successcirclecoaching.com/valuesaudio and in Appendix A. You will need at least 20 minutes of undistracted time to complete this exercise. You will also need a timer if you are not listening to the audio version of this. *It is important to do this exercise before moving on in this book.*

As you go through this list, remember that you have the choice whether to judge or not. We invite you to set aside the judging part of your mind and trust your gut as you do this.

Use the worsheet to write the words you connect with in the first part of the exercise. First impressions are important so write down all of the words that you feel a connection to. Each word you choose reflects what's important to you.

Go now to the audio version at www.successcirclecoaching.com/valuesaudio and press play, or go to Appendix A.

Step 1

Step 2

Now take a look at your list, set your timer for 90 seconds and choose your top 10 values:

1.

2.

3.

4.

5.

6.

7.

8.

9.

10.

Step 3

Set your timer for 1 minute and from your list of 10 pick your top 5 values.

1.

2.

3.

4.

5.

Step 4

Last time! Set your timer for 45 seconds. Now, take a huge breath and ask yourself: "Which three, from the five above, most represents what I honor in my life, what is most important to me and reflects who I am as a person." Choose your top 3.

1.

2.

3.

Your Core Essences

While <u>all</u> of your values are important to you and play a part in your life, these 3 values are your core values. These are the essence of who you are as a human being, and by honoring them, you respect who you are as a person. Your core values, or core essences, are the power source that will rejuvenate you when you live by them.

Michael Angier writes in his book, *101 Ways to Be Your Best,* "When we are clear on what we want, clear on our core values- on who we are and what we stand for- there is no stopping us."

Am I Living By My Core Values?

How do you know you are living and honoring your values? Think about a time when you struggled, felt like you were suffocating or were working so hard and not getting anywhere? Take a minute and, painful as it may be, really call that situation to mind. Now look at each of your top 3 core values and consider how each one played (or didn't play) a part then.

When we are not being true to ourselves, we feel like we are living someone else's life.

One of the ways to know if you chose the values that are core for you is to imagine you had to live your life without that value. If you immediately think, "No way I would not feel like me", you've probably identified a core value.

Giving up that part of your life would feel like giving up breathing. If you think, "No big deal"– then that is not a core value.

Think about the times in your life when you were in the flow; when you felt energized and alive. Where is that happening in your life now? Do you recognize the presence of your core values?

Your Core Values and Your Sphere

Take a moment and look back to chapter 2 and the key words you wrote on page 38.

Write those words here:

_____

_____

_____

_____

_____

_____

How do these key words compare to the core values you just identified?

_____

_____

_____

_____

_____

_____

Take a moment to notice where you are honoring these values. Notice where you are not and how that feels. No judgment, just notice. Entertain the possibility that you can shift from judgment to curiosity. Try these questions as a way to switch from judgment to curiosity: "I wonder why..."; " I'm curious how it would be different if..." or simply "What if...".

Overwhelm

If there are any areas on your Personal Thriving Sphere where you feel a sense of overwhelm, it's most likely because you are not honoring one of your core values. It might be that in this area you are tolerating certain circumstances because you do not feel in control. These usually do not benefit you or your family in the long run. You'll find much more on this in Chapter 9.

Thomas Leonard in the *The Portable Coach* referred to these "tolerations" as energy drains. If you feel that your energy is being sucked right out of you with certain activities or people in your life, you may not be living true to your principles. Be brave and dare to be honest with yourself about this. You'll feel it.

Knowing what your core values are gives you a tuning fork or a measuring stick to use to make decisions and to change where you expend your time and energy. In the next chapter, we will play with how to use this awareness of your core values to create a refreshed vision.

Keys Ideas for Thriving

- Identify your core values
- Identify where in your life you are living by your core values and how that feels
- Identify where you are not honoring your core values and consider how you might shift your energy so that you are in line with your values.

Next Steps

For the next 30 days, live in a space that honors your values. Ask yourself daily if you are listening to your core when you make decisions. See what shows up for you.

Go to www.thrivingmothers.wordpress.com (Blog) and share your thoughts with us about your core values and what differences you are noticing in your life when you consciously honor them.

CHAPTER 4

Creating Your Vision

Just don't give up trying to do what you really want to do. Where there is love and inspiration, I don't think you can go wrong.
— Ella Fitzgerald

Once you have identified your core values, you're ready for the next vital step — to create and write your vision. Creating a vision is different from setting your goals (which you will do in chapter 6). Your vision includes how you want to be and how you want to feel, and doesn't necessarily have a specific time frame like goals do. Going through life without a vision can be like going on a trip and just driving around without a direction or destination in mind.

We have experienced this over and over in the writing of this book. Like right now. We can't write an authentic chapter about Vision without having one! No map, no trip! We each see beyond the actual writing and putting the words on the page to having the printed book in our hands. It's gorgeous and feels solid and electric to hold it at last! Beyond **that** we see this book making a difference in the world in an area that means a lot to us. Our vision is that women from around the world will read this book and will follow the exercises and use the tools to help them create more joy and happiness in their lives. We can see Moms (and women in general) losing the idea of having to balance and do it all, and instead looking for support and ways to blend the areas of their lives. We see a community of women coming together and instead of arguing, blaming or competing with each other about the different decisions we make, we come together to support and encourage one another on a deep and meaningful level. This vision is very real to us and helps propel us forward in setting our goals and then taking the action steps to help us realize this vision.

Having a relationship with your vision is what will keep you on track. It includes how you want to feel and experience the trip. It's the bigger picture of what you're really up to in your life and needs to be something you can see or feel but perhaps can't quite reach YET.

Think back to when you were inspired about something. Even for a moment, you could see it and feel it and could tell what it would be like to have it. That is what we want you to remember in this chapter, for your life and your business.

You can create your vision for any area of your life or for your life as a whole. Use your Personal Thriving Sphere and see if there is any area of your life that jumps out first. It might be the area that you most want to change or it might be the area where you have the most energy invested. Some of our clients find it useful to write a vision for each area of their lives and then blend them into a complete whole. Do what feels easiest and most useful for you.

Crafting Your Vision

Your vision begins with your dreams, your hopes and your desires for your life. This is not a pass/fail assignment. It's not possible to get this wrong. Your vision will be uniquely yours and will be fueled by your passion – something that cannot be faked! We have often heard from clients that they are afraid to write their vision because they do not know how to make it happen, or they feel like they can't possibly achieve what they can imagine.

We ask that you trust yourself for the moment and let go of all those worries and concerns. This is not the place to be concerned about how you are going to get there. Creating your vision is fun and playful. It will be the script for your journey. So let's start with your dreams — and we are going to invite you to DREAM FREELY!!! Not necessarily big, but freely. Set 'em loose! Go back to some of the dreams you may have forgotten; those you had in childhood perhaps.

"The vision must be followed by the venture. It is not enough to stare up the steps, we must step up the stairs."
Vance Havner

Making it Fun

Below are different ways to get your dreams out into the
open. Each of them involves having fun and being playful.
Choose one or try both:

ONE

Grab some paper and a pen you enjoy writing with. Find a
quiet space and start to write about all your dreams and desires.
If you have a hard time getting started, you may want to begin by
making a list of some things you'd love to do while you are alive.
It could be the *100 Things To Do Before I Die List* or your *Someday,*
Maybe List (how often have you said: "Someday I would like to ," or
"Maybe if I had the time or money, I would "....). You get the idea.

Quiet the voice that says you can't have what you want. Give it a
graham cracker and send it outside to play. Remember what you used
to daydream about as a child. Allow your mind to flow and capture
all of the thoughts that come to you. Let yourself have the enthusiasm
of a child as you write about what you want or what you would like to
create. You may want to draw pictures or use colors to liven up your
writing. You can also use stickers or cut out words from a magazine to
help you create your vision. Get as specific as you can about what you
desire. Use plenty of detail.

TWO

Try making a Happiness Board.

Scott Martineau in his book, *The Power of You*, adapted and modified the work of Dr. David Viscott and presents the concept of using a Happiness Board to help you get in touch with your vision. To create a Happiness Board, you will need the following materials:

- 2 x 3 foot tag board, poster board or a bulletin board
- Note card size sticky notes
- An assortment of markers

Write all of your hopes and dreams in short phrases on the sticky notes. Scott offers the following fill in the blanks as helpful:

"*I want to*_____"

"*I hope to*_____"

"*I dream of*_____"

"*I love*_____"

Continue to complete this for all areas of your life. Keep placing them on your happiness board and notice how you feel. Place each of the cards in categories so you begin to see a picture of your vision. Notice which cards line up with your core values, how you feel and how you <u>want</u> to feel in the future. What would you want for yourself in each of these areas? Write this out as your vision.

Write yourself a letter

In this next exercise, we are asking you to play with a time frame for your vision. Imagine it is one year from today. How would you like your life to look and feel? What has shifted? Where are you? Who's with you? What do you love about what's happening? What/who have you let go of? Go ahead and have fun with this. You can imagine whatever you want.

Use all of your senses. Describe in vivid detail how your house looks, how you feel about your business or what activities your family is involved in. Make it REAL. If you are not feeling passionate about what you're writing yet, if you can't feel how it will impact your life, be brave and dig deeper, woman. The more vivid it is, and the more emotion you feel when you read it, the more power your vision will have for you.

Now, write this as letter to yourself. Date it one year from now. Write what is happening in your life, how your business is thriving, how your family is growing and how you are blending all the areas in your life. **Send it to us at vision@successcirclecoaching.com and we'll send it back to you one year from now!**

Putting it all in Focus

Your vision, fueled by your passion for your life and your work, will move you toward a thriving life. Before moving on to create your Passion Statement in the next chapter, you need clarity about where you want to go. Keep playing with your vision until you have a connection with the journey you want to be on. Go back to your Personal Thriving Sphere and notice if each area is represented in your vision. Notice where you have plenty of energy, and also notice areas you may feel you SHOULD be doing something so you wrote it down. If you lack energy and enthusiasm in a certain area, ask yourself if you want to continue doing what you have been doing. Perhaps a shift is in order. The power is yours, whether you believe it or not yet!

Key Ideas for Thriving

Your vision is not a destination, it's a journey and an experience.

Connect with your desires and dreams in a playful way.

Tap into your passion. You've got to feel it to make your vision happen.

Next Steps

Go to www.thrivingmothers.wordpress.com and share your dreams and visions with us and the Thriving Mothers' Community

Re-visit your Personal Thriving Sphere and see if your energy or time commitments have changed. Complete a new sphere if it has been more than 30 days since the last one you completed or if you feel you have made changes. You may also want to create a PTS based upon your Vision and date it one year from now.

Get ready to create your Passion Statement.

CHAPTER 5

Your Passion Statement

Enthusiasm is the most powerful engine of success.
When you do a thing, do it with all your might.
Put your whole soul into it. Stamp it with your personality.
Be active, be energetic, be enthusiastic and faithful,
and you will accomplish your object. Nothing great was ever
achieved without enthusiasm.

Ralph Waldo Emerson

Vision in Action

Now that you've written your vision, how can you take it into action?   If you were starting a business plan, your first step would be to create a mission statement.
A mission statement is a kind of distilling of your vision. It asks these three questions: Who are you? What are you doing? And why are you doing what you're doing?

Steven Covey, in *The 7 Habits of Highly Effective People*, talks about making a personal mission statement when he discusses his 2nd habit, Begin with the End in Mind. We liked this idea very much, yet it felt a bit like something we would create for someone else to judge us by. "State your mission." We had the sense that by creating a mission statement we'd have to prove or defend it, and what we really wanted was to create a statement that would express and stand for the best in us. So, to shape this into a meaningful tool for women, we're calling it a *Passion Statement* — a declaration of our deeply connected personal mission.

The Container of the Passion Statement

Are you hesitant to set goals because you've done it before and it "hasn't worked"? No matter what you do, you never seem to get there? If you looked back at your journal entries from a year ago, would you notice that you'd set an intention or two that has not yet come to be? Well, why not? Was your heart not in it? Perhaps you set this goal without really believing you could have it. Perhaps you set it for someone else and not for yourself. Maybe you are not even sure why you wrote it in the first place.

If you have been following the book and doing all of the exercises, this is what you have accomplished thus far:

◉ You have established the main areas of your life through your Personal Thriving Sphere[SM];

◉ You've identified your **values** as your compass to ensure you are following the road that you want and not taking detours;

◉ And you have investigated your **vision** and written it up as a map.

When I stand before God at the end of my life, I would hope
that I would not have a single bit of talent left, and could
say, "I used everything you gave me."
— *Erma Bombeck*

Great. But, what if you started out on this journey, and
weren't sure why you were headed in a certain direction.
Maybe you just forgot. Maybe you're not sure you ever
really knew why you set out. Your passion is that Why.
It is the fuel that keeps you going in the direction you've
chosen, even when you may come across some roadblocks.

Really, what you are creating when you write out your
Passion Statement is your own unique set of rules and
limits. These covenants, whether you are aware of them
or not, are your friends. Maybe even your mentors. When
you are thriving, these will be where you refer to make
a decision. Much like creating a mission statement for a
business, you can create a Passion Statement as the matrix,
or context, of why you want what you want. Why you do
what you do.

Creating Yours

We often hear from clients that either they are not passionate about anything or they are passionate about too many things. If you fall into the first group, begin with what gives you energy. What makes you feel happy or open? Is there something you do where you lose track of time? Is there any cause or issue that you are particularly enthusiastic about?

As Jack Canfield writes about in his book, *The Success Principles*, passion is something inside you that provides you with continued enthusiasm. He notes that the origins of *enthusiasm* are the Greek word *entheos*, which means "to be filled with God". Enthusiasm and passion come from deep down. They are not something you can fake. It's your authentic fuel. Your unique way of "being filled with God". When you are passionate about what you are doing and know you are following your purpose, your path is easy, clear and you attract to you the tools and resources you need along the way.

If you find that you are passionate about too many things, go back to your values list and see which truly support your core values. Also look to see if there is a thread or a theme that connects all the activities you are passionate about. For instance, say you are passionate about your health, a vibrant community and the environment. Perhaps the connector among these would be Well-Being, rippling out in wider circles to encompass your community and the environment. Often you will find your passion in what your areas have in common at their core.

Tools To Help You Write Your Passion Statement

These exercises will support you in writing a statement that taps into your values and purpose and connect with your WHY!

First tap into each area of your life and ask yourself "what do I love about this?" Examples might include:

- ◉ What do I love about my relationship with my family?
- ◉ What do I appreciate most about my business?
- ◉ What excites me about my community?
- ◉ What do I love to be involved in?
- ◉ What environment do I enjoy being in most?
- ◉ Whom do I enjoy spending time with? Why?

The purpose of life, after all, is to live it, to taste experience to the utmost, to reach out eagerly and without fear for newer and richer experiences.
— Eleanor Roosevelt

Passion Statement Sorting Tool

Take a little time in a quiet place and fill this in for yourself

1. When my life is thriving, I am _____,
   and I feel _____.

2. When my life is thriving, I am _____,
   and I feel _____.

3. When my life is thriving, I am _____,
   and I feel _____.

4. When my life is thriving, I am _____,
   and I feel _____.

5. When my life is thriving, I am _____,
   and I feel _____.

6. When my life is thriving, I am _____,
   and I feel _____.

7. When my life is thriving, I am _____,
   and I feel _____.

8. When my life is thriving, I am _____,
   and I feel _____.

9. When my life is thriving, I am _____,
   and I feel _____.

10. When my life is thriving, I am _____,
    and I feel _____.

◉ Much like we did with the Values exercise, you'll now hone this down to your top five. Starting with the first two, chose which of these is most important to you. Which one brings you the most joy and makes you feel the most complete. If you could only have one or the other, which one would it be?

◉ Trust your first impulse. Be open and let yourself be surprised.

◉ Continue through the list until you have chosen your top five.

◉ Now bring them all together and craft these top five into your Passion Statement. It can be a sentence or two, or it can be a whole paragraph.

Here is "Beth Ann's", Passion Statement as an example:
My passion is to thrive and to view the world and those around me from a place of abundance. I am dedicated to having freedom and flow, creativity, beauty and appreciation in my life. My passion is to be an entrepreneur whose relationships and parenting are enhanced by the clarity and power I feel in my working life. I am a woman who values integrity. My intention is to do business and interact with people who are honest and act out of integrity. I am dedicated to supporting others in creating and living a life of abundance, passion and purpose.

Yours can be shorter if you wish. This statement sums up what ignites and fuels our lives and work. It is what keeps us moving forward with purpose and joy.

Check out *The Passion Test*, by Chris and Janet Attwood for more ideas.

4 Simple Ways to Put Your Passion into Action

To develop a deeper relationship with your Passion Statement, get to know it well by using it daily. It's who you are in a context that helps you thrive. Feel it turn your engine over and help you drive forward. Nothing fuels you more than acting out of your passion.

1. Write it daily. Spend a few minutes in your journal each day writing your Passion Statement out. Let it evolve.

2. Keep the statement visible all around you. Write it on index cards and place it by your computer, on your bathroom mirror, as a bookmark in the book you are reading, or anywhere else you spend your time.

3. Let it in. When you read, or even when you bring to mind your Passion Statement, stop whatever you are doing. Pencils down. Place a hand on your belly and take a long slow deep breath.

4. Notice what happens. When you have a choice or decision to make, take 10 seconds to notice if you are honoring yourself by calling on your Passion Statement. What do you feel?

Let It Grow

As you begin to sharpen your awareness of whether your thoughts and actions are in alignment with your Passion Statement, you plant a profound seed of personal truth. You'll start to recognize when what you think and what you choose to do is empowering or disempowering you – increasing or decreasing your energy. It is when you are not living in your purpose and connecting with your passion that struggle and overwhelm set in. In the next chapter we will be supporting you to take the forward moving actions by setting your goals. Women who dare to claim passionate goals can make a huge and meaningful difference in the world.

Key Ideas for Thriving

When you are connected to your passion, you are able to create enormous amounts of success because you are fueled with your authentic enthusiasm.

When you feel struggle, re-assess whether your thoughts and actions are connected to your passion. Notice and honor how you feel.

Next Steps

In Chapter 6, you'll be exploring and setting some goals. We invite you to commit to plant your goals, like seeds, in the rich soil of your Passion Statement.

You may want to re-fresh your *Personal Thriving Sphere*^SM now that you've written your Passion Statement.

Go to www.thrivingmothers.wordpress.com and share with the rest of your community what is your passion and purpose. We invite you to make a declaration of this.

CHAPTER 6

Go Go Goals

Congratulations! You've got your vehicle for the trip (your Personal Thriving Sphere and Values); you've got a map and a destination (Vision) and you've got fuel (your Passion Statement). Time to get in the car and GO on the first leg of the journey.

> Whether this seems very easy, or seems very hard, you're right. It will be what you make it.

Go is the first part of the word Goals. It's time for the rubber to meet the road and get into action on something that matters to you – personal, professional, spiritual or social.

Now, we've seen just the word **goals** itself have a paralyzing effect on people. We hope to offer you a different experience here. Whether this seems very easy, or seems very hard, you're right. It will be what you make it.

> *You may want to try a different word than goal.*
> *How about Target. Aim. Endeavor.*
> *Ambition. Objective. Purpose. Aspiration.*

Find something that feels like a good fit for you so you can relax and move on to setting them in motion!

We like to view goals as the mileage markers on our journey. They let us know we are following our map and moving toward our destination -- our vision. Goals connect, flow from and manifest our passion and excitement! They are there to inspire us and serve us, not enslave us. Goals are our buddies – like the ones who actually show up and help you on moving day — and they help, really truly help, make things happen!

There are mounds and mounds of resources on goal setting out there. (We know! Each of us has a mound of them in our offices!) You can dig into more of this wealth of material if you want or feel you need to. In this chapter, we are going to help you create your goals in a very simple and effective manner.

We can't solve problems by using the same kind
of thinking we used when we created them.
— Albert Einstein

Follow Your Passion

Here's the basic steps you'll take:

1. Choose one thing you'd like to change or accomplish.

2. Make the commitment to move toward that.

3. Create a plan.

4. Start taking action (one step at a time).

5. Ask for support along the way.

Deciding What You Really Want

Bring out your Personal Thriving Sphere[SM] and for each area of your life, ask yourself:

◉ What would I do in this part of my life if I absolutely knew I would succeed? Dream freely. Allow yourself to honor and reconnect with your core values.

If you have trouble answering that question for any area, perhaps that area needs to be shifted. Take note where you want to change the activities you are involved in. Once you have something for each area, ask yourself:

◉ Where is my biggest dissatisfaction and my biggest yearning? Where am I feeling pushed and where am I feeling pulled?

This is where you will be most motivated to make a change. Trust your first impulse. The one you feel in your gut. As a matter of fact, take a moment and place your hand on your belly and ask yourself, "Is this the goal I'd like to shoot for first?"

Once you've got a <u>yes</u>, write that down.

Now, take a nice, long, slow deep breath.

Make a Commitment to Yourself

Even goals that seem small require a commitment to see them through. So, ask yourself:

⦿ Am I willing and excited to commit my time, energy and money (if needed) to reach this goal?

If you cannot answer yes, you are not committed to that goal. Try changing an aspect of it, like the time frame or amount, and check again. Still not answering with "yes"? Choose a different goal. It is better to stop and know this is not the goal for you NOW rather than several months down the road when you are experiencing resistance and struggle. If you feel that way about one of your goals, it may be one of those plates you have been spinning that you need to put down for the moment and take a look at later. It may be a plate you've been spinning only because you think you should.

Make a Plan

Try this simple tool for mapping a plan for getting from where you currently are to your goal.

⦿ Start at the top and fill in the My Desired Outcome section. Describe how you will feel, what will be in place, how things look, sound, smell. This is the place for juicy details. Use the present tense. (For example: It is April 10, 2008 and I am...)

◉ Next fill out the bottom section – My Current Situation. This is a place to describe what is so right now. Try to leave out the judgment and just state the facts. (For example: I have one client).

◉ Begin the center section – the Action Plan – by looking at what you've listed in your Current Reality Situation and Desired Outcome sections and ask yourself "What needs to happen to get me from where I am to where I want to be?" Then start listing the tasks in the left hand column in that section (you may need more paper for this later). This will be practical steps like "write flyer copy", "get gym membership", etc.

Make your steps small and doable. ("Write flyer copy" rather than "Finish entire marketing plan".) If they feel too big or you are beginning to feel resistance to taking action, ask yourself if you're trying to make a quantum leap, or if this is the right time to take this on. Check in on your commitment to this goal.

◉ Fill in the middle column of the Action Plan section for each item in the left hand column. How do you want to feel about this task? Yup, you have a choice. How you want to BE as you write that article? What environment would support you to meditate each day? Consider the feelings you want to choose around each task.

◉ Fill in the right hand column for each task. How much time would you like to allot to this task? Another great question to ask is "How long is this REALLY going to take?" We may have been putting off making a phone call so it seems like it would take a month to call that person. In reality, it probably really will take you all of 10 minutes. Great. When will you do it? Write that down here, too. Yes!

Remember, you don't need to accomplish all of your action steps at the same time. You may find that some steps overlap. Leverage your time and energy and blend the areas of your life together. Forget trying to balance everything at one time.

◉ You can then rearrange your Action Plan list in order of priority. Like we said, you might need some more paper.

◉ Enjoy mapping the dynamic flow of your goal! Show this to someone else who could get excited with you!

The Dynamic Flow Chart

My Desired Result

Where I am going.

_____

_____

_____

_____

_____

Action Plan

Building a bridge from where I am to where I want to be.

Tasks	How I Want to Feel	Time I Give This & When I'll DO It	Priority

My Current Situation

Where I am now.

_____

_____

_____

_____

_____

Ask For Help

Start with one burning goal. Don't try to do your whole life at once! As you get a feel for this, or if you are ready to bust out in another area, do this same process for each area and go for it. Thriving requires nurturing. Take exceptionally good care of yourself in this process.

As you are setting your goals, see where you might need help. This may include continuing education for needed skills, or you may need someone else's talent. Heck, you might just plain want some support and encouragement. We invite you to include all these needs into your plan. Knowing when you need help and then asking for it is one way to practice what we call Radical Self Care. We will be speaking more about this in later chapters.

If you have taken these steps, we want to stop here and deeply, sincerely acknowledge you for your bravery and willingness to change. You have truly committed to your success by identifying and beginning to take action steps. Your resources have been identified and you ready to activate them. We invite you to include the Thriving Mothers' Community as one of your resources for support and encouragement (and even perhaps some talent). Consider us part of your team.

Key Ideas for Thriving

- Be passionate about your dreams and goals.
- Commit to yourself!!!
- Set doable action steps.
- Include how you want to feel as a vital part of your Action Plan
- Identify resources and ask for help!

Next Steps

Put all of your exercises where you can easily look at them every day.

Take a look at how far you have come to this point. How are you thriving? What about your family? How is your business doing?

Share with the Thriving Mothers' Community at www.thrivingmothers.wordpress.com. We would love to read about your dreams, goals and accomplishments as well as offer additional tools and support.

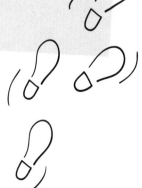

Possible Roadblocks and Detours on the Road to Thriving

In the first section of this book, you've created a strong foundation of what's working well in your life and where your center is. Now you've got a whole toolbox for thriving. Congratulations! So, what about those days when you feel not quite thriving yet? The next few chapters are dedicated to how to recognize when you're off track. You'll also find generous resources for reconnecting with the Thriving Mother inside you.

Read these chapters through now, even if you're feeling on top of your game. Then keep the book handy for those days when you need a little help from your friends.

CHAPTER 7

Lack of Control—Let Go!

Have you got that feeling of losing control creeping in? Do you feel a hum of stress under everything? Like the car's moving, but you're not the one driving? Feeling lack of control is a very common way we experience being off center.

Often this state of mind shows up when we are trying to control too much. We're trying to spin plates that are not ours to handle. Yeah, yeah, we know, you think you can get it done much faster than anyone else. You think the whole thing depends on you. You think in order to get it done right, you've got to be the one to do it. How's that working for you?

Tool #1

Setting Short-Term Intentions

You can get a fresh perspective by getting clear on what your intentions are. Really, intentions are a way of reconnecting with what's most important to you. It's a way to start something with the end in mind, to focus on your desired outcome. And it's a way of quickly refocusing on you being the center and in control — rather than trying to get your bearings from external circumstances which you have no control over.

Let's say you've been busy all day, there's a huge amount on your plate right now and you walk into the kitchen to make dinner with the house in chaos. You start to get things out of the fridge and drop a carton of eggs on the floor that somebody didn't put away properly.

Stop. Resist the urge to begin yelling at the nearest human (or pet). Scream to yourself if you need to.

Now, breathe.

Ask yourself what's important to you about mealtime.

Regardless of how anyone else behaves, how do YOU want to feel for the next half hour?

Now say your intention out loud. It may be something like – "At the end of this half hour, I'll have a hot yummy meal on the table, and I intend to feel calm and amused at how seriously I was just taking myself."

Imagine how that mealtime will be now that you have a different perspective and feeling. Instead of being frustrated and annoyed, you will be able to enjoy that hot, yummy meal with your family and feel GOOD inside and out. And they will too!

We invite you to begin your day setting intentions. Before you even get out of bed in the morning, envision yourself back in bed at the end of the day. Scan quickly in your mind what you have scheduled for the day. Don't begin a mental "to do" list. Just imagine yourself going through your day. Now ask yourself, "How do I want to feel today?" or "How do I want my day to flow?" You might want the day to be fun or productive. You may want to feel inspired, connected, calm and the list goes on. We bet you'll never say to yourself, "I want to feel out of control and frazzled today."

Take a small action to make your intention a reality.

Once you are connected to how you want to feel throughout your day, determine what you can do to support that intention. Again, the small action steps make all the difference in how you experience your life. So, if you want to feel calm about getting the kids ready for school, what will help you to feel calm? Perhaps getting up 10 minutes earlier will give you that extra time you need. Planning ahead will allow you to send them off with a smile and a hug instead of them rushing off to catch the bus with a "Bye, Mom" and a quick wave of the hand as they run out the door.

As you go through your day, check in with your overall intention. Are you on or off track? If feeling calm was your intention, and you feel anything but calm, check in and ask, "What in this moment will help me feel calm?" Maybe you need a moment to breathe; maybe you need to laugh at yourself, or perhaps a quick phone call to your best friend will put you back on track.

Setting mini-intentions for whatever you have scheduled throughout your day helps it flow in a much more conscious way. This can take 15 seconds. Really! First identify what you need to do, determine what you want the outcome to be and how you want to feel, and then state this out loud. Try this for anything you're feeling uncomfortable or irritable about doing. A phone call you've been putting off. Doing your taxes. Driving in traffic. How do you want to feel while you're doing it and how do you want to feel when it's done?

Thriving P.S. – You can do this for things that are fun or enjoyable, too! In fact, we highly encourage you to use intentions in all areas of your life; you might find that more and more tasks become fun and enjoyable just by setting clear intentions.

Tool #2

The Responsibility Spread Sheet

Are you feeling like you're doing everyone's share of the work? Do you get frustrated when people don't do what they said they would, or you fear that they just won't. Sort out what's yours and what's not with this simple little chart.

Make six columns.

◉ First column – list the event or task that needs to happen.

◉ Second – What you are responsible for?

◉ Third – What you are not responsible for?

◉ Fourth – write in the other person or people in the relationship.

◉ Fifth – What they are responsible for?

◉ Sixth – What they are not responsible for?

You can print out more copies of this form @ www.successcirclecoaching.com/resources.

Here's an example for the task of making calls to invite people to look at a business opportunity:

Event or Task	I AM Responsible for:	I AM NOT Responsible for:	Other Person in Relationship	They ARE Responsible for:	They ARE NOT Responsible for:
Phone Invitations	Making the call Being authentic Inviting from my passion and belief Being respectful and not pushy	Their presence on the other end Their timing Them saying yes or no Their response to my opportunity.	**Invitee**	How they're feeling Letting me know if this is not a good time to talk Their own response Letting me know if they're interested	How I'm feeling Pleasing me by saying yes Doing what I want them to do

Look deep inside and truthfully determine what is yours to own and what is not. When you take responsibility only for what is yours and not someone else's, you gain a sense of control and a sense of release — control over the areas that you can change and where you can take action; and a letting go in those areas that are not your responsibility. WOW — how freeing is that?! Now you don't have to spin someone else's plates. You can focus on and make choices about your own plates. You can plan how you take action, how you react to situations, and you can determine what outcome you want.

This chapter has been about putting you back in the driver's seat. If you take a look at your Personal Thriving Sphere^{SM}, you will remember that we put you in the center right in the beginning. You set the tone and pace for each area. As the hub of your own wheel, you get to determine how you want to experience each area of your life and how you want to blend your time and energy. You can stop reacting to what is happening to you, and start to take back your power of choice. You'll find yourself playing a lot more, perhaps even catch yourself humming a tune once in a while. The point is, you'll have more fun and enjoy life much more being in control than out of control.

Key Ideas for Thriving

Feeling lack of control often comes from trying to control too much.

When you're feeling out of control, get clear on what's yours to handle and what's not.

Be willing to let go of trying to spin it all!

Remember to focus on how you feel now, how you want to feel when your day is done, and how you can support that feeling and intention throughout the day.

Next Steps

Go to www.thrivingmothers.wordpress.com

Notice what you are letting go off and how freeing that feels. Enjoy!!

Notes

Stop Spinning Plates!

CHAPTER 8

Are You Should-ing On Yourself?

In Chapter 7 we talked about control — when you are feeling in it and when you need to let go of it. We introduced the concept of setting intentions, and hopefully you have practiced using them. And we presented a very vital key to thriving — identifying who is responsible for what and letting go of "stuff" that is not yours.

Hmm. Letting go of the stuff that is not yours. That is a big step. A lifelong practice, really. We honor you if this is a place you tend to get stuck. When we ask moms why they do all that they do, we get answers like these:

◉ I am the ONLY one there is to do it.

◉ I am supposed to handle it all.

◉ That is my job and responsibility.

◉ I don't know — I have always done it this way.

We hear a lot of shoulds from moms, and we would like to offer an alternative. It is the source of most of the stress we see in our clients, our friends and in ourselves. Why is it important to change this endless circle of Should? Because it's like a snake eating its tail – all you do in the should zone is go around and around, stuck and frustrated, justifying why you're doing what you're doing. Driven by what others will think of you. "I'm supposed to." "I should know better." "I should have learned by now." "I should be getting different results with the same thoughts and actions I've been hanging on to for decades!" Whew! Isn't it time to stop "should-ing" on yourself?

This Should-ing has a heavy hand in our lives as mothers and we think it's worth taking a deeper look at. As moms, we often take things on because we think we, subtlety or not so subtlety, Should. This feeds our feeling of being out of control – since we're being directed by something outside of ourselves. It's tricky though, because it feels like it's our stuff – or like it should be! When are we going to be free of it?

Should Conditioning

How we've been brought up, what our beliefs are, the norms and media images of "good' and "right" are what make up our conditioning. It is almost like there is a set of laws filed away in our subconscious minds which controls our entire lives and runs the Should department. If there's a place we can make dramatic change in our lives, it's here. We can retrain our minds and learn to drop the judgments on ourselves and on each other.

Just to be clear, we are not talking about being irresponsible or only doing what you feel like doing in a tra la la kind of way. We are talking about becoming aware of where you are sourcing your energy for your daily life.

The first way to make a change is to notice when you are judging yourself and others. Whenever you notice yourself thinking "I should be doing this or that" — STOP!!

Take a moment and ask yourself -- Why? Where is this coming from? What is making me think this? And what do I want to do, or how do I want to feel instead?

So, Why am I Doing That Again?

Go back to your Personal Thriving Sphere^{SM} and your values. Are there areas of your life where you are spending time and energy only because you think you Should? What would your life be like if you changed that to spending time and energy in all the areas where you had passion? What would it be like to do what needs to be done for your family from your authentic center? How much better could you serve the people you love in your life? Reconnecting to your unique meaning and purpose in the daily tasks of your life is a precious gift.

An interesting thing about Should is that we not only feel lousy when we are should-ing on ourselves; we are also not giving our best to those around us. The frustration and overwhelm seeps out from us to anybody in the vicinity – especially those we love the most. Think how much more fun your life would be if you really stopped should-ing on yourself and followed your passion instead. How would you view your family time? Anything change in your view of your business? What about how you feel about yourself?

We know, you're thinking, "But there are things in my life I <u>have</u> to do that I have no passion for." Let's see how you can change these from something you feel like you should do, to something you can connect to your core.

Let's take a look at why this worked for Beth Ann. By determining her "why" for this task and changing how she viewed her role, Beth Ann shifted the task from

Beth Ann's Example

Beth Ann feels she should do the laundry everyday and she should be responsible for every aspect of the laundry. She strives to get the laundry washed and put away every day because that is what "good moms" should do. She is beginning to feel overwhelmed because her children need her after school for homework and activities, and her own business is growing.

She knows the laundry still needs to get done, but she starts to see she can change how she is feeling about it. She decides to try not doing ALL the laundry herself. She thought it was her task and her task alone. WHY?? She realized that she likes doing things for her family and she likes her family to have clean clothes. However, when Beth Ann takes a look at her values, high on her list is play and family time. Somewhere along the line, she lost track of that.

So Beth Ann changed doing the laundry from a task which was overwhelming her to a task that allowed her to blend the areas of her life and include her family.

First, instead of just placing the clothes in her sons' rooms and then nagging them to put them away day after day, she began to spend 5 minutes with them putting away clothes after school. Beth Ann talked to them about their day as they put away clothes. It allowed her to spend one-on-one time with each of them, and they received help doing a chore they did not particularly like doing. Each of them also had exclusive Mom time.

At first there was grumbling and mumblings from both sides: Beth Ann thinking "I should not have to help put away these clothes" (again with the should) and from the boys who did not want to stop for 5 minutes and put away their clothes. However, within a week, this all changed. For the boys, they had time to spend with Mom when they had her complete attention and they were no longer being nagged about the clothes. It often took less than 5 minutes, so they had time to look at a project they were working on or read part of a really cool book.

something that would overwhelm her to a task that brought her closer to her family and actually brought her energy. She learned how to blend the areas of her life and connect them instead of trying to balance them as distinctly different.

Choice and Vitality

We invite you take an area of your life and change how you are doing it. One of the major benefits of changing your Should to a want is the feeling of being in choice. When you make your own choices, you will naturally feel more in control and thus feel better about the energy you are expending. You may find a well of vitality and energy you didn't even know was possible!

She learned how to blend the areas of her life and connect them instead of trying to balance them as distinctly different.

Generating Shoulds for Others

Here's something to really look at – you generate Shoulds for other people. In learning to take these compassionate steps for yourself, you must also recognize that judgment is a form of Should. When you are thinking that other people should, or should not, be doing something, you are passing judgment on them. Think what would happen if, instead, you got curious about them and felt compassion toward them.

Again, this is a lifelong exercise and is at the true core of all the world's religions! The Golden Rule; pretty big stuff that we human beings have been working toward for thousands of years. You can tap into that and really change your energy, the energy of the person you were judging and the world around you just by stepping into a place of curiosity rather than the place of judgment. Go on, we dare you. Spend one day trying to understand the Why instead of should-ing on yourself or someone else.

The Golden Rule. Treat others as you would like to be treated yourself.

Setting Rules and Limits

When you feel like you don't have a choice, your life feels like its happening <u>to</u> you. That is why your name goes in the center of your Personal Thriving Sphere^{SM}. You **are** the center of your own experience and you can activate this awareness in all areas of your life.

How do you make the choices you want to make? One way is to determine the rules for your life. Oh man, I need to make up rules? Yep, you do. Rule is actually a four letter word that supports you and your vision for your life. You'll set your rules not to hinder or confine you, but to free yourself!

It all begins with your values. What rules can you implement in your life that will support your values? Mary set herself a rule that proclaimed the weekday hours between 3 and 8 PM as Family Time. She gets the majority of her work done in the time her son is at school or after he's gone to bed. This serves her value of time richness with family. Mary has implemented this without feeling the need

Rule is actually a four letter word that supports you and your vision for your life.

to defend why she is doing it. She lets her clients and colleagues know what her work hours are and they honor that. She does not schedule meetings for this time and if she gets a call, she allows her voicemail to pick it up. There are no thoughts for Mary that she should be doing something other than what she is doing at that moment in time. Mary is honoring herself, her work and her family. By doing so, she feels excited and refreshed during her working time and her clients get the best of her. During her family time, they get the best of her because she is not thinking about what work she should be doing instead. Mary is in choice and in control. (She's doing a Happy Dance right now to celebrate!)

Rules Banish Shoulds

Take the time now to look over the areas of your life where you don't feel in control and you are doing things because you feel like you should. Do any boundaries or rules come to mind that might free you up here? Put yourself back in control. Without blaming or judging, make a rule that supports you and your family. Let others know what it is. There is no need to defend what your rule is. Just claim it and ease into it. Look for ways to blend different areas of your life.

Key Ideas for Thriving

When you do something just because you think you should, you are not honoring your values and this contributes to a feeling of being out of control.

Start thinking of ways to blend the areas of your life rather than seeing them as distinct and separate.

Step into the place of curiosity and away from judgment of self and others.

Next Steps

Go to www.thrivingmothers.wordpress.com and share your shoulds. Ask for support in shifting them to wants instead. Share what is working for you.

Create at least one rule that will support your values and change a should in your life to a want.

CHAPTER 9

Overwhelm—
It's All About Lack

Along the journey you will have various kinds of detours and what we call side trips. Some will be mildly distracting; others may be pretty intense and throw you way off track. The difference is the length of time it lasts and the impact it has on your life. When you have taken a really wrong turn, lost your map or forgot why you began the trip in the first place, you have landed in the place of overwhelm. There is something really fundamental that needs to shift.

Once you're in a place of overwhelm, you're no longer connected to your vision. It doesn't seem to matter anymore. Here is what you might notice:

◉ Rushing from task to task.
◉ Feeling like you are not sure what to do next because there is so much to do.
◉ Feeling like your head is too full.

◉ Being tired to the point of not wanting to do anything.

◉ Questioning your abilities*.

Being disconnected from your vision is common and can happen at any point. However, we often see it in our clients at the 3 month mark. We call it the 90 day slump. It seems that about 90 days into a new business or a new project, there is a decrease in passion and energy. This is when we often hear the question "Why did I start this in the first place?" The initial excitement and enthusiasm has worn off as the work sets in. The honeymoon is over. This is where many women who start home-based businesses often feel themselves wanting to give up and quit.

So, are you ready to lose your balance and get out of overwhelm and back to thriving?

Overwhelm occurs because, as women, we have been programmed to keep everything "in balance". So, are you ready to lose your balance and get out of overwhelm and back to thriving?

·······································

We want to acknowledge honestly here that these can also be signs of something physical or psychological going on that is beyond the scope of our book or our training. Please recognize that if things are really dire for you or your family, there is professional help out there for you, and we urge you to find it. The information in this book is not intended to replace the care of a professional.

What's Working?

Ok, grab a cup of coffee or tea and let's take a few moments to look at what is working for you. Instead of looking at what is going on, pick one area you would like to change or feel better about. Got it? Great!! Now, what is one thing that is already working well for you in that part of your life? Even if it seems insignificant right now, name it. You may want to go back to something that was previously working. Is it still working or do you need to do something different?

We are asking you to make a major shift from Problem-Solver to Thriving-Thinker here. It's going to feel great, so stay with this. We're asking you to focus on what is already working well so that you can build on your strength in that area. It ain't broke, we don't have to fix anything here.

Next question — What is it that makes that thing work so well? Why does this work for you? Notice which of your core values show up in your answers.

Take a moment to notice how it feels to focus on what's working. Save the "yeah, buts" for now and really let in how this feels for you.

Creative Leveraging –
It's NOT Multi-Tasking

¹le·ver·age

Pronunciation: 'le-v&-rij, 'lE-; 'lev-rij

Function: *noun*

1: the action of a lever or the mechanical advantage gained by it

2: power, effectiveness

Now we're going to turn your What's Working into a creative lever for how you use your time. Leveraging time is a valuable and underutilized resource. It is not the same as multi-tasking. You may think you are being ultimately productive when you multi-task, but you are not. Multi-tasking is actually an energy zapper. It is a myth. You cannot truly do two things at once. Every time you switch from one task to another, your brain switches from one part to another. Women's brains are really good at this. These are nanosecond switches back and forth that are occurring over and over again as you multi-task. The effect is an increase in energy usage and decrease in focus.

Ever wonder why you feel so tired at the end of a morning where you have been "great at multi-tasking"? Have you ever taken a moment to stop when you have 3 or 4 activities started and wonder what you're doing and what you have to do next? You lose focus. Think about how many accidents are occurring because people are driving and talking on the phone. The ability to truly attend to two tasks at once is a lie.

So what is leveraging all about? It is taking two (or more) areas of your life and blending them so that you use your resources wisely. For Sue, one example has been the incorporation of Dream Dinners* into her life.

Sue hated 4-6 PM every day with a passion. She would begin to feel anxious around 3 PM trying to figure out what to make for dinner. It was a huge energy zapper and began to spill over into how she felt about other areas of her life. She knew she needed to do something. She had tried other solutions but none felt right for her. So she went back to her vision of mealtime for her family. Her vision was that she would prepare hot meals that her family liked, and that she had a part in preparing and cooking. Here is what else Sue wrote on her want list:

◉ To know ahead of time what I am preparing for dinner at least 4 times a week
◉ To know how much time each meal takes to cook so I can prepare and make them with ease
◉ To spend more time with my kids when they get home from school and daycare and less time spent rushing around in the kitchen

···

*Dream Dinners is a franchise, started by two women, that provides menu planning, shopping, prep-work and clean-up by moving the meal assembly process out of people's kitchens and into specially equipped stores. www.dreamdinners.com

Her solution was the opening of a Dream Dinners in her community. Sue has leveraged her time and now prepares a month's worth of meals in about 90 minutes. When she first started, it would take about 2 ½ hours, which was still great. Sue was able to make meals that her family liked and she was saving a ton of time she used to spend preparing the meals as well as food shopping.

Then Sue decided she wanted more social time in her life. She invited a friend. They go together every month and help prepare each other's meals. When they work together, talking the whole time, it only takes 90 minutes and they spend the rest of the time socializing with each other. They also chat with the owner and employees, so it's a mini-community. This is a regular event for them which is planned and FUN. It has helped Sue become more creative with her meal planning. Since she is no longer striving and struggling to get dinner ready and on the table, mealtime is now a thriving time in her family's life. It is in alignment with Sue's vision to have a shared family meal which she can also enjoy. This allows her to focus more on her family. (Sue is doing the Happy Dance now!)

Your Turn

It's all About Blending

Let's take a look at what you want to leverage and what resources you can draw from.

What do you want to change?

Why do you want to make a change?

What is your vision of thriving in this area?

How will you feel when you are thriving?

How can you leverage your time, energy, money or community to make this happen easily for you?

Most likely you will also be supporting someone else's goals and vision at the same time. Women helping women — that's what it is all about.

When you feel like you have gone off track, always go back to the center of your wheel. Yep, that is your name there. It always begins with you. Use the tools to support the foundation you created in Section 1 of this book. Stop trying to do more with less. Multi-tasking and trying to cram more into a day does not work. If you continue that pattern, you will soon run out of gas and feel rather empty. We will be exploring that in the next chapter.

Instead, identify the areas where you can blend and leverage your resources so they support you. Most likely you will also be supporting someone else's goals and vision at the same time. Women helping women – that's what it is all about.

Key Ideas for Thriving

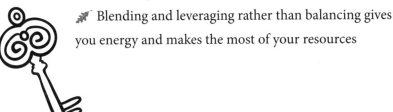

🍁 Multi-tasking does not save you time and is not an effective way of being

🍃 Focus on what's working well already and use that to create leverage!

🌿 Blending and leveraging rather than balancing gives you energy and makes the most of your resources

Next Steps

👟 Go to www.thrivingmothers.wordpress.com and share how you are using blending and leveraging. You may also get some great ideas as well.

👟 Help expand our community by inviting a friend to become a part of it.

👟 Make a commitment to stop trying to balance it all.

Notes

CHAPTER 10

Stress and Fear

> The most important decision we make
> is whether we believe we live in a
> friendly or hostile universe.
> — Albert Einstein

Ok, so you're past the point of feeling a little hectic. Everything seems to be **way** too much and those plates are threatening to crash. Some of them may already have. You can't seem to get a grip. HELP!

We hear you and help is on the way!

Here's the interesting thing, when you feel like life is too much, it is really because of a sense of lack. Even though a lot seems to be happening, the stress comes from the fear of not having enough time, energy, money or support. That's when you freak out. Right?

It's as if your gas tank is empty and you're determined to continue your massive road trip. You're making choices and decisions from an empty tank, and certainly not enjoying the effort! What are you going to run on — fumes? How could you possibly move even an inch let alone go on for miles? Welcome to downtown Stressville!

Pull over, woman.

Time to fill 'er up!

The devastating effect of too much stress on our bodies, minds and hearts is well known. Living stressfully depletes us on every level. It comes to us in so many ways – worry, information overload, unhealthy diet, relationship issues. Get curious about yourself and learn to recognize your unique signs of approaching stress. Gather your own research on what happens to you when you're headed past overwhelm.

Fear – The Bottom Line

Everything we've covered in this section – feeling out of control, should-ing, overwhelm — really comes down to fear. Perhaps you fear change, success or not belonging. You might, at the bottom of it all, really fear letting people see who you are, fear losing your identity or have the fear you might somehow jeopardize your role within your family or community. All of this can cause your energy to slowly and continually become more and more depleted. When you are running on fear as fuel, it's like there's a hole in your tank — no matter how you try to fill up, just as much fuel runs right out into the dirt.

We want you to know right here and now — there is nothing wrong with you if you are afraid! Hey, you're human, you get scared.

It can be helpful to recognize that fear has a role in informing you about what is important. It's a messenger. Fear can be your friend and ally, if you learn to hear what it's saying to you.

There are several things FEAR can stand for: **F**orget **E**verything **A**nd **R**un; or **F**alse **E**xpectations **A**ppearing **R**eal; or how about **F**rozen, **E**ndangered **A**nd **R**eacting.

Even if you can only access a glimmer of remembering that you are the center of your life, you can make a choice right here and now. Maybe you could have a laugh at how FEAR could change to **F**ree **E**verybody **A**nd **R**espond. Or **F**eeling **E**nergized **A**nd **R**eady. Whatever FEAR means to you, notice how it is affecting your life, and start to imagine what you would like to do instead. In order to do that, you need to stop and patch the leaks. Stop and take time to ease the fear. Then you can replenish your fuel and your tank will fill again.

See if these tools help. Since this is a time to take a step back and take it easy on yourself, the resources we are offering here are <u>very</u> simple:

Tool #1

Breathe, baby

Take three long slow deep breaths. Let the air fill all the way to the top of your lungs under your collarbone. Let it out slowly. Try hissing the air out and imagine a pressure cooker letting off steam. Do this often and whenever you just need a moment. You might try setting a (non-irritating) timer in your office or kitchen and let it be a reminder to breathe each time it goes off. Get one of those wall clocks that sounds a bird call on each hour. When the bird sings, let it be a reminder to take three long breaths.

Tool #2

Absolutely Nothing

Find a place to sit down where there is less distraction. Find your own quiet corner, or even go outside if there's a quiet place nearby. Sit. And for at least 30 seconds do absolutely nothing. Yup, just 30 seconds of nothing. No special breathing, no intention setting, no journaling, no watching TV – nothing. Be like a wise old woman in a rocking chair on the front porch. Rest your hands on your lap. Just watch. Just breathe. Just be.*

Tool #3

Simplify – Take One Step

Notice that often what paralyzes you is feeling like you have to do it all. And it's all or nothing, right. Clean the whole house, or don't do it at all. Finish the list of 20 phone calls, or do none of them. Make a list of 10 things to do, check off 8 of them during the day and obsess over the 2

···

*Thanks to Teresa Romain for this one.
www.accessabundance.com

you didn't do all night long. It's the not enough thing – either there's not enough time, energy or money, or you're not good enough to get it right. This is scarcity thinking, friend.

Let's replace this with a bit of abundance and simplicity. Apply what we call a One Step. Take. One. Step. Make one call and then acknowledge yourself for it. Notice how you just treated yourself by doing this. Notice how compassionate it is to do a One Step move and then celebrate. Try it. You get to be your own best inner-mother. "Nice job, honey. You're doing great! I'm so proud of you." Also take a One Step when you want to let go or make a change. Instead of feeling like you should get it all completely shifted today by 3 o'clock, take One Step in the direction of your goal. Now celebrate! Repeat! One Step at a time.

Get Support and Coaching

This is where coaching can be very helpful, to move beyond the places you usually bump up against fear and stop yourself. A professional coach is a partner on the journey and can help you create the space to move beyond your fear in a way you just can't get there alone.

You can also reach out to your community. You have gained a tremendous community just by reading this book. Connect with other women on the Community's blog www.thrivingmothers.wordpress.com or by participating in the Thriving Mothers' Community Calls. Look for opportunities in your local community to reach out for support. In the next section we will talk more in-depth about how you can give and receive support from your communities.

Check Your Gas Gauge

Now take a moment to notice – is your tank full? Or is it ½ full? Maybe it's only got a few drops of fuel in it, and if that's the case, don't plan to do something like re-design your entire website today! First, congratulate yourself for being **aware** that your tank only has a few drops in it.

Put your hand on your heart right now and acknowledge yourself! Come on. Let it in.

Great! Now that you are aware, you have choices. You could choose to replenish your fuel supply right now. You could take this time to do one of the simple tools in this chapter. Or you could choose to do a task that only takes a few drops of fuel. It is truly up to you. Awareness leads to choice. Choice helps you create a life that thrives.

We're so proud of you!

Key Ideas for Thriving

🍁 Try to do just One Step to create forward movement

🍂 When you are aware of and honor how you feel, you can create more choices for yourself.

🍃 Reach out for coaching and support – try the Thriving Mothers Community for starters

🍁 Breathe, baby.

Next Steps

👟 Right now- BREATHE and see how that feels. Repeat as Needed!

👟 Go to www.thrivingmothers.wordpress.com and share your ideas for re-fueling.

Step Into your Greatness

From Survival to Thrival Mode

What a journey! You've identified what is important to you and created a vision and goals to live into it. You've looked at some of the dark shadowy places in your soul and what holds you back. This is what it's taken for you to survive.

Now we like to invite you to step into your true greatness and celebrate it. Not anybody else's idea of your greatness, your own truth. This next section of the book shifts away from looking at your roadblocks to embracing the parts of the journey where you thrive and where you help others to thrive.

Think of how you feel when you recognize growth and maturity in your children—sometimes in huge ways, and in sometimes very small but significant ways. You get to enjoy that same pride and delight in witnessing yourself expand into your potential. Breathe it in. Soak it up. Savor it. Let your life thrive!

CHAPTER 11

Identifying Your Strengths

> "Greatness may take the form of a great endeavor, or it may manifest as a fullness of life – a living out of one's Essence self – Essence is neither a place nor a time, an insight or a state of mind. It is the deepest part of our nature, an actual presence that is innate and inborn. Absolutely everyone has the capacity to be great, but few notice or own it "
> — Jean Houston

Your Inner Greatness

What are the qualities of your inner greatness – your essence? As women we can certainly carry with us the message to not blow our own horns. It may be very uncomfortable or unfamiliar to recognize your awesomeness. But you **are** awesome. Every single one of you is awesome; each in your own way. So, what's that way for you? Are you a great listener? Can you hear and sing harmony? Do you have the patience to watch a child learn to write in cursive? Are you funny? Can you organize and inspire people?

Mary sees her greatness in her ability to bravely go right to the heart of what really matters to a person or to a group. She is great at blending the masculine and the feminine, and sees that as one of her unique roles on the planet. She is also really in touch with her creativity, imagination, humor and connection to nature. These things combine to make her a dynamic leader, teacher, guide, mentor and coach for deep, soulful, meaningful change. And a really fun person to be around!

Sue sees her greatness in her ability to listen with her whole being; to identify individual and group beliefs that support and hinder them. She is able to inspire others to get out of their own way and stand in their greatness and she stands there with them, supporting them all the way. She brings to her relationships the knowledge and belief that anything is possible for anyone. She utilizes play and creative thinking on a daily basis which allows her to be an inspired leader, facilitator, teacher, coach, mentor, wife and mother. And a really fun person to be around!

Now you know why we collaborated on this book. We are both really fun people to be around and we bet you are too — if you let yourself be that person.

The potential and capacity in you, in all of us, has barely been tapped. Let's tap it together! Sometimes we just can't see what we've got in us. We need someone else to reflect it back to us.

As soon as you trust yourself,
you will know how to live.
— Johann Wolfgang von Goethe

Harvest the Seeds of Your Greatness

Try this — Ask five friends, family and acquaintances what they see as your strengths. Be humble and let it in. Don't deflect it away. Just listen and say thank you. Notice how their words most likely reflect your values.

The world needs you to BE your greatness. It matters. You matter. Who you are in your fullness is needed right here and now – in your life, your family, your community and the world. If you don't believe that yet, just trust us for now.

Try this — Write your autobiography, decade by decade. Don't feel like you have to write the great American memoir, just note what important events have shaped each decade of your life so far. Include what you have learned as you've navigated your life's ups and downs. Notice and celebrate your accomplishments and milestones. Share this with a friend, or do it with a group of women!

Your Own Definition of Greatness

Try this — Choose one role or area of your life, like, say, Motherhood. Now take some time to explore what being a great mom looks or feels like to you. Perhaps you have seen this greatness in someone else. When have you seen it in yourself? What brings it out of you? How does it feel when you see or experience this way of being?

Uniqueness

There is nobody else like you in the world. In business, we often talk about finding your niche, or target audience — the group of people you are uniquely suited to serve. Recognizing and serving your niche can bring amazing focus, clarity and fullness to your work. Rather than trying to provide for (or please) everyone, you give your finest to the people you can best assist or support. Those you are **meant** to serve. This is when your heart really sings.

So. Who are your people? What is it about you that is uniquely suited to serve them? What does this say about you? One more question. How does it feel to pay attention to how exceptional you truly are?

There is a vitality, a life force, an energy, a quickening
that is translated through you into action
and because there is only one you in all of time,
this expression is unique.

And if you block it,

it will never exist through any other medium
and it will be lost.
The world will not have it.

It is not your business to determine how good it is
nor how valuable,
nor how it compares with other expressions.

It is your business to keep it yours clearly and directly
to keep the channel open.

— **Martha Graham**

Power

Let your greatness and uniqueness dwell in the core of
your being, and what you'll get a taste of is your own
power. You are powerful force of nature. We're not talking
about dominating-over-others kind of power; we're
talking about vitality-strength-and-wisdom kind
of power.

We're talking about the most precious of all our powers
– the power of choice. Once you start to really understand
that you can choose how you experience anything that life

brings your way, you are living in your power. Your power of choice is your freedom. Living from the center of your life, you can respond rather than react. Wooo! We can feel it moving up in you even just reading these words. It's moving in us, too! When we remember this, and especially when we help each other remember it, anything is possible!

Can you feel how much we need this in the world right now?

Reminding one another of the dream that each of us aspires to may be enough for us to set each other free.
— Antoine De Saint-Exupery

Taking Care of Your Treasure

You are a valuable treasure. There's a great story about a rumor that gets started in a monastery that the Messiah is one of the monks living there, but no one knows which monk it is. It may even be them! So, they all begin to treat each other with a great honor and respect as if each person is the potential Messiah, and the community thrives.

We've given you lots of tools already to help and support you to know and be good to yourself. Now we're going to up the ante and recommend what we call Radical Self Care. Find the things in your life that nurture and fill you up in a deep way, and make them a habit in your life.

Your Legacy

Try this – this is a very powerful exercise! As if you were at the end of your life, write your parting words. You may want to do this as if you were writing your speech to read at your 100th birthday party. You could write your own obituary as you would love it to be read at your memorial service. Some folks have actually thrown themselves a party before they died and celebrated with those they loved and got to hear what people would say! Include forgiveness, humor, and what you hope to leave behind for the next generations.

Being With Your Greatness

Now that you have acknowledged what your capacity is and have begun to embrace your greatness, what are you going to do about it? How can you put on, almost like a suit, this person with great wisdom or humor or creative thinking? The Possible Woman. The Thriving Mother.

We invite you to put that suit on for the next 30 days; be your greatness, or your vision of greatness. If you are not quite comfortable with it all yet, try what we call Acting As If. Make your business decisions from your place of greatness. Interact with your children and family members from this place and see what happens. Allow your strengths to serve you and help you serve.

Key Ideas for Thriving

Greatness is more about being than doing.

Fully owning your greatness allows you to serve others in a bigger way while supporting your true self

By using your strengths, you will thrive and so will those around you.

Next Steps

Get ready to recognize and BE a champion

Go to www.thrivingmothers.wordpress.com and share your greatness, uniqueness, power and legacy.

CHAPTER 12

Connecting: Community, Networks and Champions

If your vision is for a year, plant wheat. If your vision is for ten years, plant trees. If your vision is for a lifetime, plant people.

— Chinese proverb

Welcome to an exhilarating and meaningful part of your journey – choosing whom you'll travel with. In Chapter 10 we introduced the idea of checking the level in your fuel tank. If you don't feel fully engaged yet, we invite you to look at those tools again. Ready? Time to get connected and make a difference! Let's explore how other folks can help you fill your tank, and how you can support them to fill up their tanks – just by being who you truly are.

Imagine you have a secondary fuel tank of resources we'll call your "Community Assets". It is these Community Assets (CAs) that you exchange with the people whose lives you touch. Your Community Assets might include your editing skills, the people you know from a previous work environment, your ability to counsel people in trauma, your creative way of teaching math to teenagers. The possibilities are endless when you really start thinking about it. When you offer your wisdom, gifts and talents to your community and network, you tap into your CA supply to help fill their tanks. Then, when you need the wisdom, gifts and talents of others, your Community Assets tank gets filled by their contributions to you.

So whenever you open yourself up to receiving from someone else, you also give them the gift of being able to give.

Giving and Receiving

When you are engaged in any relationship, there is give and take. As mothers, we are often good at the giving part and sometimes not as good at the receiving part. This relationship is Yin and Yang because whenever someone gives, someone else has the opportunity to receive. So whenever you open yourself up to receiving from someone else, you also give them the gift of being able to give. Here's something amazing, your tank gets filled either way. When you ask for support you get filled up — because of what is given to you and because <u>you allowed somebody to give.</u> When you give to others, you get filled up because <u>you were needed</u>!

The reluctance to receive can show up in several different ways. Perhaps you are not sure what you need, so you are not sure how to ask. Perhaps you don't want to "bother" another person by asking for what you need. Or you don't feel like you "should " ask for anything and you "should" do it all yourself. Maybe you don't want to feel indebted to someone if they help you.

The Law of Attraction is: *That which is like unto itself is drawn*. Basically, what you put out, you get back. It's an abundant principle that assures us that there's plenty to go around. So, keep filling up your Community Assets tank by asking for what you need or want help with and you'll have plenty to give to others when they need something you're good at.

Who's Who?

Take out your Personal Thriving Sphere, and if updates are in order, pull out a fresh sheet and do that first. Now, look at each area and begin to notice who is in your network or community related to each part of your life. Who do you know from your business, who do you know from your kids' school or activities, from your spiritual life and so on for each area? Don't think about HOW you are going to ask for help. Just brainstorm who is in your network. Write them all down.

This is how you get to know who is a part of your network and also to get your network ready for action. The word "networking" may feel easy, fun and like something you love to do.

Or perhaps the thought of networking is like having a tooth pulled without novocaine. No worries, wherever you fall on this spectrum, we intend networking to feel both doable and enjoyable for you by the end of this chapter.

For now, think of networking as connecting; connecting your greatness and what you have to offer (your CAs) with those who could really benefit from it. AND connecting YOU to what you may need. It's like an old fashioned barn raising, when all the neighbors came over and your barn went up in just a day. If you tried to do it alone, it would be months. When you utilize your network effectively you enrich your relationships and expand and deepen your sense of community. You belong.

My Connections

People I know connected to each part of my life:

Area 1 _____

Area 2 _____

Area 3 _____

Area 4 _____

Area 5 _____

Area 6 _____

Area 7 _____

Area 8 _____

Brainstorming to Fill Your Tank

Now, let's fill up your Community Assets tank so you are up to date on the resources you have to draw from. In order to fill up the tank effectively, you need to recognize and celebrate your gifts and talents. Begin with what you learned about yourself and your strengths from the last chapter. Now answer these questions for yourself:

1. What type of thinker am I? Am I creative, analytical, big visionary, detail oriented....

2. What books and magazines do I like to read?

3. What organizations (recreational and professional) do I belong to?

4. What is my educational background?

5. What do I do really well?

6. What is a skill I have that I'm really proud of?

7. I feel energized and playful when I am_____
_____.

8. In my free time I like to _____
_____.

These are all ways that you can add to the energy and resources of your community, network, project, family and friends.

Connecting the Dots

Think about your business (or other project or personal growth you are working on) and note what you love about it and why. Go back to your vision and see where your business is now compared to where you want your business to be. What is not yet in place for your business to thrive? Write down all the things you might need to make your business ideal for you. Which things do you already have in place and which ones do you need your network for?

Are you an organized and structured thinker? Perhaps that supports your community when you help organize a school fundraiser or you create the sports' schedule. You are probably already offering to your Community Assets without realizing it. You are filling up the tank and you can also draw from it. For example, you might be great at creating systems for your business because you are organized and structured. However, you are stuck in creating your marketing flyer. You need a creative, outside-the-box thinker. This is when you go back to your network list and see who in your community has that talent and skill and ASK them for help. If someone does not immediately come to mind, ask those in your network if they know someone who has the skills you need. The beauty of your network is that it ripples out way beyond just your inner circle.

You may not fully realize the strength and the depth of resources that already exist in your network. Ask the people in your network these questions and allow yourself to soak in the bounty of the strengths, talents and uniqueness that already exists for you to tap into.

Champions — Your Greatest Asset

A strong and vital community - no matter how you define it — is essential for thriving. Being a champion for yourself and for others brings that thriving to a whole new level. The definition of a champion is:

One who engages in any contest; especially one who in ancient times contended in single combat in behalf of another's honor or rights; or one who now acts or speaks in behalf of a person or a cause; a defender; an advocate; a hero.

Being a champion for yourself is about knowing your strengths, believing in your vision and enlisting the support of others for you and your cause. This can occur in all aspects of your life. For the moment, we are going to talk about enlisting champions for your business. If you don't have a business, pick another area of your life where you are passionate about growing.

Are you currently a champion for your business? Do you believe in yourself unconditionally? Do you advocate for your business?

◉ How would <u>you</u> define the word champion?

◉ Where in your life would you benefit most by seeing yourself as a champion?

◉ What would it feel like to approach projects or personal challenges as a champion?

Now that you have a sense of what it looks and feels like, what three actions are you going to take this week to support your business like a champion?

Exercise

Order Form for a Champion

Write a description of your ideal champion. How will she or he support you? What strengths will she or he have? What change will occur in your business once you enlist a champion's help?

Take a look at your network to find one person you could enlist to completely support and advocate for you.

How about two? Hmm — what about three people? WOW! What amazing results you will have when you have members of your community lobbying for you and your success.

Pass It on

We invite you to be that ideal champion for someone else. What would it feel like to be a champion for someone you truly believed in? Where can you support another woman's business, project or change?

Expand your Community

You may be thinking only about your local community as your network. We invite you to think bigger and more globally. Each of you is a member of our Thriving Mothers' Community and perhaps you have already posted to our blog or participated in our community calls. If not, we invite you to add us to your Community Assets tanks and when you need, tap into the resources that are here.

Key Ideas for Thriving

Networking is about connections and relationships.

You have assets and resources you can offer to your community and also receive from it – your Community Assets.

Become a champion and advocate for yourself and for others.

Next Steps

Add to your global community by posting to your Thriving Mothers' Community at www.thrivingmothers.wordpress.com

Get ready to regain your balance in the next chapter

Notes

CHAPTER 13

Revisiting Balance — Harmony

> When one door of happiness closes, another opens; but often we look so long at the closed door that we do not see the one which has opened for us.
> — Helen Keller

What if we saw the many plates of our lives not as burdens, but as exciting parts of ourselves that we get to experience? The difference between stressfully surviving and enthusiastically thriving is in our perspective. It's how you think and talk about it that matters. Not just to you, but to all of us. We can turn what we "have to" do from a burden into a joy.

We're not talking about just putting a happy face on everything; we're talking about rising to the call of our capacity as women! Look what we get to do as women at this time on the planet. We have a greater potential for meaningful lives on so many levels than the previous generations of women did. Our mothers and grandmothers didn't have these opportunities! What if we saw the many roles we play not as a source of stress, but for the exciting gift of hugeness it is. We are needed in this world!

Your Own Version of Thriving

We hope that by this time in the book, you have really stepped into the knowledge that YOU are the center of your experience, and that you have choice. It is in that place of choice that we thrive. We get to choose how many plates we spin, how fast and when. Like plants and animals, we have cycles in our lives. There are times when we are flourishing with growth and activities, and are feeling vibrant and able to take on the world. There are other times, when we want to quiet the growth to reflect on our lives and where we are heading; when we want to expend our energy into one or two vital tasks or activities that will support our overall being.

For each of you, thriving will look different. And **that** is awesome. Diversity rocks. Step into the place of thriving that is right for you — a place where you are able to evolve at your own pace, where you are able to make mistakes and "do it all over's". Instead of having to live up to some false vision of what a woman and mother Should be; choose the type of woman you want to be, and BE her. Connect to your passion and your greatness and LIVE that. LIVE that for yourself, your family and your community. Support other women to live in their greatness and support their desire to thrive.

Revisiting Balance

So when we say Lose Your Balance, we're not saying the word or concept of balance is bad. It's the way we saw it affecting us all that we wanted to challenge. In fact, we like the definition of balance as being in harmony. When you are thriving, you are in harmony with your true self, and thus in balance. Not spinning plates because you are supposed to, for some reason you can't put your finger on.

Our Journey

Mary and Sue have learned a great deal about thriving throughout the journey of writing and experiencing this book. We have noticed when we felt like we were going out of "balance" trying to "balance" too much. We noticed when our heads felt so full of information that we could not expend energy on simple decisions, like how to get our hair styled (that was Sue), or what in the world could we possibly have for dinner (that was Mary).

We have utilized <u>all</u> of the tools we've created and presented here. Not just because we wanted to check them out – we really needed them! We have deepened our personal connection and exchanged bushels of Community Assets with each other and on behalf of this project.

What you leave behind is not what is engraved in stone monuments, but what is woven into the lives of others.
— Pericles

We've stayed up all night in hotel rooms so we could be together and collaborate in person. We've breathed in the space of what it felt like to thrive as a partner, entrepreneur, mother and woman. We've tapped into greatnesses that neither of us knew existed when we began. Both of us experienced losses and tremendous wins along the way.

The connections we make with incredible women when we talk about thriving and being in choice has continued to fuel our passion and fill our tanks. We notice the light that goes on in their eyes, and their breathing into a bigger space that happens when we talk about thriving instead of "doing it all" or having to be "everything to everyone".

We have fully embraced that this is a journey, and that thriving is a choice. We invite and encourage you to embrace this choice as well.

Here's to the adventure!

Key Ideas for Thriving

🍂 Thriving is a choice.

🌿 You can be in harmony with yourself and with your life.

🍂 This is a great time to be alive as a woman!

Next Steps

👟 Go to the appendix for additional resources and recommended readings.

👟 For your free thank you gifts see page 173.

👟 Go to www.thrivingmothers.wordpress.com and continue your journey of thriving.

Appendix A

Thriving Values Profile^{SM}

This exercise will help you identify your core values. You will need about 20 minutes of uninterrupted time to complete this exercise. For this first part, you can either have someone read these words to you or read them yourself. Set the timer for 10 min and circle each word that you think or feel is important to you. Trust your instinct and don't spend too much time analyzing. If you would prefer to listen to this while you read along, you can download the audio at: www.successcirclecoaching.com/valuesaudio

Accuracy	Clarity	Education
Achievement	Compassion	Effectiveness
Acknowledgment	Competence	Encouragement
Adaptability	Competition	Energy
Adventure	Confidence	Enjoyment
Affection	Connection	Enthusiasm
Alertness	Conscientiousness	Entrepreneurism
Ambition	Consideration	Excellence
Appreciation	Contentment	Fairness
Authenticity	Contribution	Faith
Balance	Cooperation	Family
Beauty	Courage	Fitness
Boldness	Creativity	Flexibility
Broad-mindedness	Customer Service	Focus
Calmness	Dependability	Forgiveness
Capability	Determination	Freedom
Career	Diligence	Fulfillment
Caring	Discipline	Fun

Generosity

Gentleness

Good Attitude

Good Humor

Gratitude

Growth

Happiness

Hard Work

Health

Helpfulness

Honesty

Hope

Humility

Imagination

Independence

Innovation

Integrity

Joy

Kindness

Knowledge

Leadership

Learning

Love

Loyalty

Maturity

Mentorship

Meticulousness

Modesty

Naturalness

Nurturing

Optimism

Organization

Originality

Patience

Peace

Perseverance

Persistence

Personal fulfillment

Personal Mastery

Playfulness

Pleasantness

Politeness

Practicality

Precision

Professionalism

Progress

Prosperity

Punctuality

Purposefulness

Quality

Resourcefulness

Respect

Responsibility

Satisfaction

Security

Self-actualization

Self-control

Sensibility

Simplicity

Sincerity

Skill

Sociability

Specialness

Spirituality

Status

Strength

Success

Sympathy

Tact

Talent

Teaching

Teamwork

Thankfulness

Tolerance

Trustworthiness

Understanding

Uniqueness

Value

Versatility

Victory

Warmth

Willpower

Wisdom

Wit

Youthfulness

Zeal

Once you've finished this part of the excercise go back to page 45 and finish the rest.

Appendix B

Excerpts of Interviews with Work At Home Moms

Since this book was inspired by women's stories of working from home, we wanted to include short excerpts of some of our interviews.

Here you'll find:

⦿ a little about each woman,

⦿ tips they offer to women who may want to consider working from home

⦿ and what would be a meaningful legacy for each of them to pass on.

Contact information for some of these inspiring women on the Resources page of our website: www.thrivingmothers.com/resources.

Aoife Gaffney

Financial Services

"I like making something happen for someone else, making people's lives easier. I do what I'm good at and help people with their money so they can do what they're good at."

Mompreneur Tips:

◉ Don't wake up in a bad mood every day. If you don't like the job you're in, make one.

◉ Don't re-mortgage your house to start your business. You don't want the added stress of personal debt.

◉ Absolutely hire a coach.

Legacy for her son:

◉ You have choices; you are the master of your own destiny. As long as you feel your mind, you're free.

Beth Landry-Murphy

Speech Language Therapist

"I love having the free time and ability to take time off to be with the kids and just be able to revamp the schedule without going through three lines of command. All my clients know I'm a mom and things can change for my kids. They are parents too, so they appreciate it."

Mompreneur Tips:

◉ Set your parameters and stick to them. Be flexible within them but make it work for you and everything else will happen.

◉ Once you have good knowledge of your product or skill, just go for it.

◉ Think about what your values are and put your work in place around them, not the other way around.

◉ Get help where you need it as soon as you can afford it.

Legacy for her sons:

⊙ You can always work later, but you can't coach your son's soccer team later.

⊙ My son said to me the other day, "Mom, it's going to be harder when I'm older and I'm a parent." And I said why? "Well, you're such a great parent; I'll never be able to be as good as you." I hope I'm leaving behind the role model as a good parent.

Bridget Fearing

Vacation Property Owner

"All of our home businesses make it so we can meet our main goal: to be able to be home with our family. We want to avoid commuting and working for someone else on someone else's terms. The flexibility is fabulous. If we don't want to answer the phone, we don't. Most of our inquiries come in by email, so we can do things when we have time.

I don't feel as dependant if I'm earning an income and feel like I'm making a contribution beyond just the mothering aspect. It's nice to keep those skills sharp. I don't want the feeling of having to ask for permission to spend money because I didn't earn any. It feels more like part of a team because I expect my husband to participate in parenting and I feel like I equally need to be participating in income. And I enjoy what I do, I'm helping people, it's fun and exciting. I'm proud of my work and it's very rewarding to read the guestbook comments."

Mompreneur Tips:

◉ As much as you can try to work as a team with someone, if you're just on your own you don't have anyone who's familiar enough with your business to bounce ideas off of.

◉ Have the moral support, have someone to cover for you if you are on vacation or just can't handle things for a period of time.

◉ Just know that it is the toughest at the outset and to give whatever business it is AT LEAST a year for things to kind of gel. Starting a business is hard enough and being a parent is hard enough can be very hard at the beginning. But if it's a business you enjoy, then it will work out. Do your best to not to make judgments during the first year.

Legacy for her son:

"It's okay, this is what I chose and whatever level of education you do or don't have is never wasted. It goes to your kids, they see that you are a multi-faceted person, that you are a person that values family and have been creative in your way of being in the world."

Catherine Camp

Realtor and Property Manager

"I really enjoy working with people. It feels great to help people find a home. I try to offer pressure free services. There's nothing like watching your kid grow up. The more that society is willing to be so supportive of working mom's the better our community and society will be. Being a mom has given me more business because of how many more contacts I have."

Mompreneur Tips:

◉ Envision your child having fun and growing and being happy and feeling connected because mom is there.

◉ See mom thriving because she's not only a mom, but she has a business and is able to do different things

◉ Be hard working, feel a sense of worth, feel that you're contributing positively whether it be your family or your work life

◉ Focus on simplicity and what is really important and really matters

Legacy for her son:

◉ That we gave our child the best childhood we could.

◉ I want him to have a feeling of self worth and contribute to the community

◉ I hope some of our values of working and improving all the time can be instilled in him

◉ I also hope that our family can get to a point where working isn't all we do

Gea Franklin

Clothing Designer

"It's given me a lot of satisfaction and joy to have my own business. I make clothes that make people feel good and beautiful. I love seeing women being excited about wearing the clothes. I like the end result. I love fabrics. I love the process of picking the colors and making the patterns. I always try to see the good in people. The clothing that I make is to support women feeling confident and happy with themselves, so they can go out and do positive things in the world."

Mompreneur Tips:

◉ Even if you're not confident about something, just do it. Don't worry if you're going to be the best or the greatest, just go out there and try. You'll get better and better.

◉ Success is 2% talent, 98% hard work.

◉ Have patience with yourself.

◉ Do what you love.

◉ Realize that you only have one life to live and don't waste it getting stressed out.

◉ Be honest with yourself.

◉ Don't feel like you need to get success the first year you're out there, pace yourself and gather information along the way.

Legacy for her son and daughter:

◉ Intention and doing things with intention can help people out by putting positive energy out in the world.

◉ Female energy is so important to have out there in the world. I want them to see that I've been able to release a lot of goddess energy in the world

◉ I would like them to say "Wow, she did a lot of good stuff for this world and put a lot of positive energy in the world and helped a lot of people."

Heather Novak

Hypno-Therapist and Hypno-Birthing Specialist

"I love working with people. I love the flexibly and working from home. I love the infinite possibilities; that it's not the same thing over and over again. I like to bring people into my energy space and not have to buy business clothes anymore. I like to have people feel comfortable in a homey environment. I feel truly me and I don't have the stress. I can bring in the simple beauty of life and let go of the big to-do."

Mompreneur Tips:

◉ Find something that is true to your soul, your passion, your love and also to have a game plan, making it viable and doable.

◉ Create all that you can through a business while still having the love and support of your family. You don't have to sacrifice one for another.

Legacy for her daughters:

⦿ "Don't die with the music still inside of you."

⦿ Follow their passion and their hearts and have a smile on their face every day!

⦿ My 5 year old says when she grows up she wants to do "hippo" therapy.

Jennifer Turco

Graphic and Web Designer

"I love my work because it's pretty. My eyes are really happy when I work. I love working for myself. I love working at home and I treasure the solitude. I love being able to work in a beautiful place. I love my clients. I love having the time to be the kind of mom I want to be."

Mompreneur Tips:

⦿ Trust your intuition and to trust yourself'

⦿ Let your business grow organically

⦿ Your business can grow a lot by word of mouth

Legacy for her sons:

⦿ I want them to know that they matter. They come first.

⦿ That they can trust themselves.

Kathy Monet-Smith

Network Marketer

"I love that it's so flexible. I am able to do all kinds of stuff with the kids.

The money is great. I love working with people. I love people that call me telling me they feel better and things are going better for them health wise. I love that I'm helping people."

Mompreneur Tips:

⦿ Set a schedule.

⦿ Set some boundaries. The line between work and family tends to blur.

⦿ Have some days that you just don't work.

⦿ Don't wait to long to get an assistant.

⦿ Look forward, focus on what's ahead.

Legacy for her eleven children:

⦿ Lot's of great memories with the kids. The memories my kids have of us doing things together.

⦿ Enjoy the moment, spend more time enjoying the moment instead of working so hard waiting to arrive.

⦿ I would have taught the kids to really love God, and value themselves.

⦿ Have the boys all know how to be good husbands and really kind caring people.

Laurie Rasch

Clothing Designer and Seamstress

"I think it's because of my values that I work for myself. The first 10 years of my working life I worked in the corporate world and I don't like that world. It's not for me. I think it's because I needed to have more creativity in my life and those kinds of jobs don't offer that. I didn't like the way people interacted. I needed something I could get up and be happy about, it was important for me to feel good about what I did and to be home with my kids. I worked a schedule around my husband's schedule so I was able to relax all day long and be with the kids."

Mompreneur Tips:

◉ Consistency is very important.

◉ Be very self directed and take the initiative to make yourself do the job

◉ Have faith in your own ability

◉ Be real about what you think you can accomplish

◉ Scheduling, figure out how many hours you're going to work and when and it's not going to be when your kids are sitting at your feet

◉ Be able to say no, don't take on more work than you know you can do in the time you have

◉ Take care of your needs.

Legacy for her son and daughter:

⦿ That I had a dream and I stayed committed to it even when there were times it would have been easier to quit and get a regular job

⦿ Staying committed, following it through

⦿ Realizing the dream as a reality

Mary Button

Network Marketer

"This was a perfect match for my personality because I'm really about trying to help people realize their dreams. I've always been a dreamer. The business that I'm in has been an incredible vehicle not only for our family, but we're able to turn around and bless others with the same opportunities. You get to know the heart and soul of the people you're working with. And I believe that relationship building, that lifting people up, is really what we're on this planet for. It just feeds my soul."

Mompreneur Tips:

⦿ Choose a mentor that you really feel like you can be real with.

⦿ Know you have the abilities and strength within. Really go deep within and trust and you will be led.

⦿ Call on whatever spiritual resource that you have

⦿ If what's in your heart is to stay at home with their children, trust that.

Legacy for her daughters:

◉ I imagine a whole new culture of people really being connected to who they are.

◉ That my children know strong centers of who they are, what their gifts are and what they have to offer to the world.

◉ A legacy of love, pure unadulterated, unconditional love.

◉ Pay it forward; it just goes on and on.

Michelle Brookhaus

Homeopath and Reconnective Therapist

"What I really love about my business and work is the help that homeopathy can give people. It's been an honor for me to be with people on their healing paths, physically and mentally and emotionally. Homeopathy has a huge learning curve, and there's just as big a curve in learning how to run a business. I resisted it for years. Now I know I can learn to grow. Now I feel more powerful. I used to feel at the mercy of not getting it. There's a lot of power in this. It gets easier."

Mompreneur Tips:

◉ Coaching is really important. Having a coach helped me keep focused. It's always tempting to say "Gee, I can't afford coaching." But then I say "Can I not afford it?!"

◉ Ask for help! I think we as women think we should be able to do it all ourselves and we can't.

Legacy for her son:

"I've done Tai Kwan Do and set goals about getting to a belt level. I don't want to just model that for my son, though. I want to create something more open. I want him to know he can enjoy the experience of living life. I want to leave behind the value of having a full and interesting life."

Milana Leshinsky,

Entrepreneur, Internet Marketing Expert

"Thriving to me is freedom. I have freedom to be home when my children need me, to be able to go to their school plays and activities. It is the freedom to build my business the way that is best for me and my family. I work the hours that are ideal, choose the projects that I want to work on and am able to create the type of business I want. My children are also aware that I own a business and it has opened up a world of possibilities in terms of their future professions. My son knows he has the freedom to choose the career path and profession he is passionate about because he has seen that modeled by me."

Mompreneur Tips:

◉ Have passion for your business. If you do not love your business, find something that you do love and do that. Obsess even a little bit about your business.

◉ Celebrate often with your family. Celebrate the business wins as family wins; like when your children have been patient when you are stressed. Make them part of the success of your business.

◉ Talk about your business with your children. Have them understand that you own a business and be a role-model for a different way of doing work beyond the 9-5 work model. Include them in the conversation when setting goals.

◉ Recognize and honor the skills and knowledge that have because you are a business owner and that you are able to share with your children such as writing a business plan or doing a presentation.

◉ Set rules for yourself that support you and your business.

◉ Think like an entrepreneur- Get a copy of *Secrets of the Millionaire Mind: Mastering the Inner Game of Wealth* by T. Harv Eker and E-Myth by Michael E. Gerber.

Her Legacy:
◉ To fill the gap for coaches between what they learn in coaching school to what it means to own a business. To have coaches treat their business as an entrepreneurial venture; as the business it was meant to be — changing people's lives while generating profits.

Sheryl Pause

Herbalist

"I love that it's mine and that I don't have to answer to anyone. I can take the afternoon off to go to the park and not have to worry about it. I can do it at my own pace and my own level. The freedom is really what it comes down to. Having the freedom to be at home gives a lot to my family. I get to watch the growth of my daughter"

Mompreneur Tips:

◉ Have a good strong support system

◉ Take the time off when you need it

◉ Take the time to nurture yourself and your family

◉ Honor yourself, your passions and what's most important to you.

Legacy for her daughter:

◉ My business is natural skin care products. Getting the chemicals out of products is a global thing we need to work on. I hope she feels the same way and that it becomes important to her

◉ I hope that she grows up believing she can do anything she wants to do and be happy

◉ I want to leave behind respect and humanity in the world

Sue Talbert

Writer, Photographer and Adoption Advocate

"Thriving to me is being able to stay home and homeshool my kids – which is really where my heart is. I want six kids all around me and no mortgage! I like being able to say that I'm as busy as I want to be and I'm content with what I'm doing. I think of my family and the things my extra income can give to them and that makes it all worth it for me."

Mompreneur Tips:

⦿ A new business doesn't get big overnight, and that's a good thing. Let it set good roots. It takes time.

⦿ Learn how to make the business work for you, not you for it.

⦿ Figure out what you want to contribute to your monthly family budget and consider making <u>that</u> your business goal.

⦿ You are unique and that is inherently valuable. I don't care if there are 100 other people doing what looks like the same thing as you do, do it. You are a treasure.

Legacy for her son and adoptive children to come:

⦿ I'd like people to say I was full of love. I hope this gives my children an example to live by.

⦿ You teach what you know. You reproduce what you are.

⦿ You are unique, you are valuable, you are a treasure.

Bibliography

Please see our website for more of our favorite links, books, programs and fun resources: www.successcirclecoaching.com/resources

Angier, Michael E., *101 Best Ways to Be Your Best: Practical Wisdom to Help Maximize Your Unique Potential*; Success Networks International, Inc., 2005.

Attwood, Chris and Attwood, Janet Bray, *The Passion Test: The Effortless Path to Discovering your Destiny*; 1st World Publishing, 2006.

Canfield, Jack, *The Success Principles*, Harper Collins Publishers, Inc, 2005.

Covey, Stephen, *The Seven Habits of Highly Effective People*; Free Press; 2nd edition November 9, 2004.

Dyer, Wayne, *Being in Balance: 9 Principles for Creating Habits to Match Your Desires*; Hay House, Inc. 2006.

Fritz, Robert, *The Path of Least Resistance: Learning to Become the Creative Force in Your Own Life*; Ballantine Books, 1989.

Houston, Jean, *A Passion for the Possible: A Guide to Realizing Your True Potential*; Harper Collins, 1997.

Leonard, Thomas J., *The Portable Coach: 28 Surefire Strategies for Business and Personal Success,* Scribner, 1998.

Leshinsky, Milana, *Coaching Millions;* Lifestyle Entrepreneur Press, 2007.

Martineau, Scott, *The Power of You: How YOU Can Create Happiness, Balance and Wealth;* John Wiley and Sons, 2006.

Wright, Kurt, *Breaking the Rules;* CPM Publishing, 1998.

Zander, Rosamund Stone and Zander, Benjamin, *The Art of Possibility;* Penguin Books, 2002.

Websites:
Dream Dinners: www.dreamdinners.com
Access Abundance: www.accessabundance.com

Mary McHenry is passionate about thriving — as a mother, as a woman and as an entrepreneur. She has built several successful home businesses, including a flourishing network marketing organization and shares her enthusiasm

for helping women truly live what is possible for them in her coaching and mentoring practice. Find her at www.CoachMaryMcHenry.com and on her blog at www.ThePowerofOurWisdom.com

Mary has been a waitress, arts administrator, grant writer, stage hand, choreographer, choir director, ski instructor and professional dancer. She is a teacher, community organizer, wilderness guide, naturalist, leader of ceremonies, singer and an avid ice hockey player.

She is a life-long student and holds numerous professional coaching certifications. Her extensive background in communication, facilitation, mediation and leadership combined with her down to earth enjoyment of life make her a catalyst for deep and lasting change in her clients. She makes her home in a cabin high in the mountains of Colorado, with her husband of 20 years, and their nine-year-old son.

Collaborating with Sue to create Success Circle Coaching and the Thriving Mothers Community is a gift in Mary's life; what an profound opportunity to support families to fulfill their amazing potential – to truly enrich the world from the inside out.

Susan (Sue) Guiher believes that when you find and live your passion, anything is possible. Sue is passionate about women stepping into their greatness and creating their way to thrive. She found Clear Path Coaching and Consulting in 1999 to connect her love for her family, and her desire to remain at home with her infant son, with her passion and expertise for inspiring others. Since that time she has blended motherhood and entrepreneurship in a way that continually fuels her desire to assist individuals and groups to succeed in their own ventures. You can learn more and continue your conversation with Sue at www.ClearPathCoach.com.

Sue is a personal and business results coach, trainer, facilitator, speaker, author and avid lover of the outdoors. She brings to her coaching over 20 years of experience in different areas of leadership and business development, clinical programming and implementation, communications, education and sales. Sue has held positions as Clinical Director, Director of Operations, Program Manager, Corporate Trainer, Communication Specialist and internal coach working on a Change Management team. She currently resides in a beautiful Bucks County, Pennsylvania with her husband of 10 years, Mike, and their three young children, Matthew, Christopher and Meghan.

Sue's love and commitment to life-long learning is

evident in her credentials and qualifications which include numerous professional coaching certifications, accreditation by several International Coaching Organizations, dual Masters' Degrees and post-graduate work in communication, human behavior and business. Sue is presently on the Board of Directors for the Philadelphia Area Coaches Alliance and in 2007 was named a VIP WAHM by WAHM talk radio. The Philadelphia Business Journal has also recognized her as a top Executive Coach.

Sue considers herself blessed. Being able to collaborate with her wonderful partner, Mary, to create Success Circle Coaching and the Thriving Mothers' Community has truly enriched her life. Sue is passionate about continuing the journey and supporting other women along their path of thriving for themselves, their families and their communities.

Before we go, please accept your

Free Thank You Gifts!

In deep appreciation of you being a part of the Thriving Mothers vision and community, we are offering you a package of thank you gifts. Please visit www.stopspinningplates.com/thankyougifts to receive them!

Go Thrive!

Sue and Mary